REFLECTIONS ON LIFE, LOVE, AND FOOTBALL

LINDA LANGE

iUniverse, Inc.
Bloomington

Incomplete Passes
Reflections on Life, Love, and Football

Cover photograph from the Henry Lefebvre Collection of the Neville Public Museum of Brown County

iUniverse books may be ordered through booksellers or by contacting:

iUniverse
1663 Liberty Drive
Bloomington, IN 47403
www.iuniverse.com
1-800-Authors (1-800-288-4677)

ISBN: 978-1-4620-3374-4 (sc)
ISBN: 978-1-4620-3373-7 (hc)
ISBN: 978-1-4620-3372-0 (e)

Library of Congress Control Number: 2011912551

Printed in the United States of America

iUniverse rev. date: 08/19/2011

To Scott
Thanks for putting up with my obsession (and the messy house).

To Pam, Del, and Carla
Fans and friends forever.

To the Green Bay Packers, past and present
And the sportswriters who covered them
My heroes.

CONTENTS

INCOMPLETE PASSES

I turned twelve in 1959, the year Vince Lombardi came to town and changed ... well, everything. Pro football was replacing baseball as the national pastime, and the Green Bay Packers were about to become the kings of football.

I embraced the Packers that year—figuratively, of course, although I longed to do so literally. My new passion transformed the way I looked at my hometown, my world, and myself. Through our shared love of the team, I found Pam, Del, and Carla, and we formed a bond that remains strong today. You probably picked up this volume thinking it was a book about football fans, and it is. It's also a coming-of-age story and the chronicle of a musical comedy called *Third and Long*. But most important, it is a celebration of that bond.

Since my friends and I were in Green Bay, Wisconsin, and not New York or Chicago, the Packers were constantly with us. Under Coach Lombardi, they were heroes, their names known nationwide. Yet, miraculously, they were accessible! In those days before shopping centers, they had to come downtown regularly. If we made the tedious journey on the East De Pere bus, we might run into them shopping at Prange's or lunching at the Northland Hotel. And we made every effort to do so.

We're not proud of everything we did. But we sure had fun.

The Packers were our Elvis, our Beatles—or at least our Ringo Starr. *If the drummer's name conjures Jim R. and Bart S., you're first of all a Packer fan.*

We pored over their biographies in the game programs, memorizing every detail. For some of us, the players represented our first contact with people from outside the upper Midwest. Just past puberty, we melted when we heard the accent of a dashing Texan or a sweet Alabama boy. (Pammy, who had a quick ear, had to be careful not to be caught imitating them.) Among the players were also the first African Americans we knew.

The Packers' influence was felt far beyond sports. The Lombardi philosophy and work ethic could be applied to every facet of life. We were fed a mix of sports coaching, religion, and family values that played well with our Midwestern upbringing.

The upright and mild-mannered Bart Starr is often held up as an example of the era. My friends and I admired Starr, but we reserved our true affections for others. We were sure that Bart would never leave his lovely wife, Cherry, and adorable son, Bart Junior, for the likes of us! With Paul Hornung, the subject of many racy rumors, and his pal Max McGee, who knew? Some day we might have a chance!

But when you're twelve or thirteen and the object of your affections is twenty-five, there's just one problem: You're bound to be throwing ... **incomplete passes**.

HOMECOMINGS

"We can talk a bit of baseball, but it's not our fav'rite sport.
And basketball's a subject where we always come up short.
We'd rather talk about the game that brought us our renown.
We love to talk pro football … it's the only game in town.

For a big-league city, this one's really rather small,
And when the season's over, there's not much to do at all.
And you can't stay drunk all winter, though it's what you might've liked.
And so we talk pro football! It's the sport that keeps us psyched."

— "The Only Game in Town," opening number, *Third and Long*

THE BEST WEEK
OF THE YEAR

I have come full circle, and it feels wonderful. Behind the wheel of my aging Honda, I'm grinning like a fool, and Pammy's sweet, round face beams back from the passenger seat. September has returned, the Packers are playing on Sunday, and we're heading for the place we still call home.

We have been making this pilgrimage since 1997. Pam and I turned fifty that year, and going home was a way to celebrate our birthdays and the freedom of our empty nests. Del and Carla still fuss because we didn't include them that first year. "But you were only forty-nine," we tell them. The truth was, we couldn't quite believe the ads that said we could buy a package—hotel, tailgate party, and a ticket to a sold-out game—for a few hundred bucks. We figured if we got burned, it would be just the two of us, and at least we'd get to Green Bay.

But the trip fulfilled its promise, and Del and Carla accompanied us in '98. Now the four of us make the journey almost every fall, and not without sacrifice. In 2003, I talked my oncologist into stopping chemo one session early so I could complete breast cancer treatment before our chosen game. In '05, Pam was driven out of her home for a month by Hurricane Katrina, returned to an intact house surrounded by two hundred fallen trees, and got on the plane for the North Country a week later with two envelopes of amazing photos. Del, who has the farthest to come, cheerfully pays what the airlines are charging—as long as she can sell just one extra house.

Over the years, we have moved into a set routine. Our time together has expanded from a long weekend into almost a full week. Pam flies into Chicago's Midway Airport on Thursday. I drive from Cincinnati to meet her there, and I always marvel that I can make the three-hundred-mile drive and arrive just in time to rendezvous at the baggage claim. We spend the night in Chicago and head slowly up through Wisconsin on Friday. We stop and search the outlet malls that line I-94, then pick up US 41 out of Milwaukee. That first year, we were so excited to be back in Wisconsin, and together, that we called out the familiar place names on the road signs we passed. *"Oconomowoc!" "Winneconne!" "Kaukauna!"* It was as if we'd suddenly begun conversing in a long-forgotten language.

Friday's dinner is filet mignon at Vince Lombardi's Steakhouse in Appleton. If you're a Packer fan and can get to the Fox River Valley, this is a stop you have to make at least once. (Del and Carla joined us the one time, and now they beg off, but Carla remarked that the filet cut like butter.) It's a decent steakhouse, pricey for small-town Wisconsin, but a bargain compared to a Morton's or a Ruth's Chris. They know the big-city tricks like showing off the different cuts of meat before you order, and the service is attentive. But the main attraction is the surroundings.

The restaurant has an arrangement with Lombardi's children, Vincent and Susan, and basically its patrons dine in a Lombardi museum. You can see portraits of Vince with his wife Marie, photos with his players, his driver's licenses from New Jersey where he coached at St. Cecilia's High School, framed correspondence, and a replica of the Vince Lombardi Trophy that is given to Super Bowl winners. (Don't forget who won the first two.) I took my son there once, and there was something extra: He looked over my shoulder to a table across the room and said, "Mom, isn't that Paul Hornung?" It was.

Dinner concluded, we're back on 41 heading into Green Bay. We get off at Lombardi Avenue. When the handsome, brick façade of Lambeau Field looms before us, we're home. Carla has met Del's plane at Austin Straubel Airport, and they're waiting for us at a motel near the stadium.

Amid squeals and hugs, we enter the room, and the best week of the year has begun.

Tomorrow we'll shop for Packer gear, hook up with old friends, and visit favorite restaurants. Kroll's, where we've been eating "butterburgers" since the sixties, is a perennial lunch spot. If we have the time, we'll hit Sammy's for pizza, double kosher salami for Pam and me. Or Titletown Brewery, located in the old Chicago & Northwestern railroad station where we started so many adventures and said so many tearful good-byes. Often we spend Saturday night at Eve's Supper Club on Riverside Drive in Allouez, with its beautiful view and adventurous menu. Jarreth, my classmate and another lifelong Packer fan, grew up to marry Jerry Haltaufderheid, son of the eponymous Eve. Today they run the restaurant together.

I'm not trying to write a food tour of Wisconsin here. But you see, I was born Jewish, and that automatically means I'm into food. My family was like that, and so is my husband's. I'm reminded of a visit to my sister-in-law that my husband, our son, and I made some years ago. Mady, her husband Leon, and the three of us piled into the car for a tour of Chicago's ethnic neighborhoods. Mady pointed out the best places to buy Polish sausage, Italian deli, Greek pastries. My son was about fifteen at the time and undoubtedly would rather have been anywhere else. Finally he groused from the back seat, "Doesn't this family ever think about anything except food?" Four voices answered in immediate unison, "NO!"

One night at Eve's, we were dining late enough that Jarreth was able to leave her post and sit with us. A group of men at the next table, intrigued by the idea of a women's football weekend, invited us to compete in a trivia game. One of them must have just finished reading a book about the Ice Bowl, because all of the questions were from that era—our era, when we still lived in Green Bay. To the men's amazement, we answered question after question correctly. Finally, Jarrie, Pam, and I capped our achievement by singing all the lyrics of the old fight song, "Go You Packers." Of course, we remember when it used to be played live, by the Packer Lumberjack Band, during every kickoff at Lambeau.

Sunday is game day, what else? We'll dress in green and gold, load on the beads and temporary tattoos, and act as foolish as everyone else out there. It strikes me every year that there is nothing in the world I'd rather be doing than to be in that place with those people.

Pam always exclaims at vendors' selling beads for a dollar a string. We got ours free, courtesy of Pam, whose daughter attended Mardi Gras parades for years. As was the custom, Reesie would remove her shirt and folks on the floats would throw her the beads—green, gold, and purple. Pam took out the purple strands *(Vikings' color, yuk)* and carried the rest to Green Bay. Now if we need new ones, we'll have to buy them. These days, Reesie goes by her full name, Theresa. She's a lawyer and a mom, and she doesn't flash her breasts in public anymore.

One year at our tour company's tailgate party, I asked the DJ if I might read a poem I had written. We were playing the Dallas Cowboys, and my verse affirmed that the Packers, not the 'Boys, are America's Team. I recited it and basked momentarily in the applause. But I didn't even get my proverbial fifteen minutes of fame, because the DJ called for a scavenger hunt, and Pam was chosen to compete. Her mission was to produce a bra. She was wearing one, of course, but could not extract it from under several layers of clothing. She struggled bravely for several minutes as the crowd looked on, and they loved her when she finally released the undergarment and waved it high in the air. For the rest of our stay, everyone we met recognized us, but that had nothing to do with my poem. "Hey," they greeted Pam, "you're the bra lady!"

If time permits, we'll visit some other remembered haunts before we leave. The first year we came, Pam and I drove by my old house and spotted the current owner, Mary, in the yard. She allowed us to go inside. Mary's teenage son asked about the Packer sticker on his bedroom closet door. The room had been mine, and I was amazed to see the sticker still in place after thirty-five years. Even more surprising was the new archway between the living room and the dining room. My mother had often said an archway would be ideal in that location. But the dining room had been turned into a bedroom for our housekeeper, so we never did the remodeling. The people who bought the house from me and sold it to Mary had visualized the same thing, and years after my mother's death they had cut the archway exactly where she'd wanted it.

Several times we've gone to Bay Beach to walk along the waterfront, but one year we also went to the small amusement park there. There have been rides and concessions at Bay Beach since the early 1900s, and during our childhood the park was *the* place to go for Fourth of July fireworks. The miniature train—once driven by my friend Judy's father—still makes its rounds at the perimeter. With no grandchildren in tow, we passed up the tiny train, and Pam and I were leery of the Ferris wheel. But we couldn't resist the carousel. It was shiny with a new coat of paint, but looked very familiar as we made our circuit. The young attendant assured us that it was the same one we rode as little girls in the fifties.

Sometime during the weekend, we may catch a drink at Fuzzy Thurston's bar out on West Mason Street, especially if it's Packer Alumni Weekend. The beautiful old men who used to be our gods will be congregating there.

PARTNERS

As I get reacquainted with my partners-in-crime, I'll introduce them to you as well. Since I'm getting personal, I've changed their names and the names of their family members. Here's what I do throughout this book: If I give out personal information or say something that might embarrass the person, I change the names. For brief mentions, or for general statements about well-known figures—Hornung, Starr, the *Green Bay Press-Gazette* sportswriters—I use the real names. As for my three partners, I told them, "I'd better give you deniability."

Pam has been my best friend for so long that despite our different lifestyles, we slip easily back into synch. To me, though, she is a study in contradictions. She'll start my eyes rolling by repeating something racist that she's obviously heard from some redneck Louisiana neighbor, yet she'll speak lovingly of an African American student who worked hard in her class. When Barack Obama was running for the presidency, she forwarded us derogatory e-mails about him. But she then purchased his books, read them, and pronounced him a good man—although not one who'd get her vote.

Pam majored in music education and taught music for several years. One class of inner-city Milwaukee students may still remember the day their young teacher stood before them and asked, "Who knows what *mf* stands for?" (Of course, she meant *mezzo forte*, medium-loud, not that other word.) After following her first husband to Louisiana, where he attended law school at Tulane, she taught mainly fifth and sixth grade in small-town schools; she retired a couple of years ago. I never saw her in the classroom, but I think she was a good teacher. I know she was one who cared.

The rest of us worry about Pam because she has type 2 diabetes that's not well controlled. She hates exercise, which is imperative for type 2 patients, and as a result, she sometimes can't keep up with us on our outings. She's a good sport about this, as she is about almost everything. She's a good sport about having to wear hearing aids that don't quite do the job. She is a good sport rooming with me on these trips. When I get tired, I become bitchy and sometimes patronizing toward her, but she always handles it with grace.

A more telling example of her sportsmanship: When her mother-in-law became ill, Pam and her husband moved into the elderly lady's house, and Pam had to assume much of her daily care. Instead of resenting this, Pam expresses fondness for Nathalie and tells us how much she misses her now that she's gone.

Pam and I were always more infatuated with the Packers than either Del or Carla, and that is apparent today. I'm the one who follows the schedule, makes our trip arrangements, and basically carries the torch throughout the year—although Carla will sometimes call me at a "Packer moment," such as Brett Favre's plane landing at Austin Straubel Field the first time he un-retired. Pam clings to the past in other ways. She still determines that she has fully recovered from a cold by trying to articulate the name of the great linebacker "Nitschke." *(Try it with a stuffy nose!)* And we both use the players' uniform numbers as memory aids for phone numbers, zip codes, and the like. In fact, if anything happens to me on our trip, Pam will remember whose jersey numbers comprise the combination of my suitcase lock and help my husband to access my belongings.

Pam is a devout Catholic who had to get permission to stand up for me at my wedding and who never misses Mass on our Packer weekends. She wonders—literally—if she will qualify to enter heaven. Pammy, if the vote of a Jew-turned-atheist counts, you have mine.

Carla has driven up from southern Wisconsin. She's the only one of us who never left the state. Now the mother of four and grandmother of three, she retains the elfin charm that captivated me when we were girls. Carla is our official photographer and historian; she brings out albums with pictures from our past trips and from gatherings of her large family. As we look at page after page of smiling, handsome people who all resemble each other, I envy her sense of belonging.

It amazes me that Carla can trace her ancestry back to the *Mayflower*. Del can follow her lineage back almost as far. In contrast, my husband and I once consulted a couples' therapist who asked us about our great-grandparents and was horrified that we knew almost nothing. Of my four sets, I could name only one—Julius and Essie April. I knew them because I had visited Essie, who lived till I was fourteen. The counselor felt this ignorance was a sign of major family dysfunction. Rather, I think it's a cultural thing. As Jews, Scott and I come from an ethnic group that for centuries has either been trying to escape from some country or getting thrown out of some country. It wasn't easy to keep up with the *mishpocheh* left behind.

Carla always had a scientific bent. As a child, she picked up dead birds from the ground and stored them in her school bag until she had time to dissect them. She majored in medical technology, and recently retired from the lab at a VA hospital. Carla is in tune with the outdoors— gardening, camping out, and dabbling in astronomy. She is conservative and frugal. This trip is one of her few extravagances, which shows how much it means to her.

Carla and I shared a childhood activity that served me well as an adult. We created our "stories," sagas that filled many spiral notebooks throughout our high school years. Carla started it with the fictional autobiography of Jack *(not Jackie!)* Hennesey of the Packers, friend of Paul Hornung and the first girl to play football in the NFL. Not to be outdone, I began the tale of Sidney Melbourne Jr., girl hockey player for the semi-pro Green Bay Bobcats. Pam and Del also wrote stories that featured them as athletes, but they didn't continue as long. Pam preferred her fantasies of serving as the Packers' team nurse!

I learned a lot about writing from sharing my story with Carla. One day she'd write the longest sentence ever, and then I'd try to top it. Our characters had fanciful names—an officious Frenchwoman was Mlle. Colette Difficile; an Australian hockey player was Gilbert Onionskin, named after a brand of writing paper and called Peel for short; and there were the sisters, Cherry and Olive Pitts. *This was a Packers in-joke: Bart Starr's wife was named Cherry and defensive lineman Henry Jordan's was Olive, so if they'd instead married teammate Elijah Pitts ...*

I got my first taste of the power of the pen when I killed off the appealing Peel. Reading that chapter aloud, I brought tears to Carla's eyes and my own, and we mourned for several days.

In 2009, prompted by the recession and family obligations, we did not meet in Green Bay. Carla used her vacation time to join her three sisters for a hiking trip in Washington State. Characteristically, she posted photos on the Internet. For months afterward, her Facebook profile picture showed her wearing a big grin, perched on a mountain peak with a beautiful valley below her. It's a classic illustration of accomplishment by a vigorous, sixty-one-year-old woman. And it totally sums up Carla.

Del is not a small woman, but she is comfortable in her body and takes care of it. When we choose a hotel, it must have a pool where Del can swim laps. It's not unusual, when we're together, for her to suddenly drop to the floor and perform calisthenics, or enter a room flossing her teeth. She lives in a small town in the mountains of northern California and alternately praises the serenity and bemoans the unavailability of upscale stores and restaurants. She did something about the lack of cultural experiences a few years ago, by helping to build a theater in her area.

California has left its mark on Del. One year she politely asked me to find a more elaborate tailgate party than the one we'd been to—one that would have some good salads! *Salads?* She works as a realtor and has a second job going into schools and teaching sex education at the behest of Planned Parenthood. She has spent much of her life on the West Coast—in the Bay Area, Seattle, and now northern California—and she followed her second husband to China for a year, at the end of which he left her for a

Chinese woman. She weathered this, raised her three children to maturity, and made a new life for herself.

Del is a strong and passionate woman. We listen with alternating fascination and horror to her stories of middle-aged dating. One year we couldn't figure out why she looked so good until she told us she'd had cosmetic surgery and shared her before-and-after pictures. Another time we learned that Del—the only single member of our group—had two boyfriends and was "getting it" far more often than the rest of us.

Del quilts, and she delights us with handmade birthday and holiday cards. Every so often we'll get an e-mail or a Facebook post from her, just a little spot of joy, with a picture or a description of a wonderful day she's had. Her politics are liberal. Although twice married, she has always kept her maiden name. Growing up, I knew Del the least of the three, but now I often find her the easiest to talk to, because she's lived in more places and has been exposed to more points of view than either Carla or Pam.

We have few secrets. Del talks freely about the impact of her father's death when she was nineteen, and how her search for comfort made her promiscuous for a while. Pam relates tales of her "eccentric" husband, who loves a bargain so much that he once brought home several cases of marked-down dog food—even though his family didn't have a dog. We share our hopes and fears for our children. When one of us complains about a husband's hurtful remark, the others soothe and support her. We are far from alike, but we rarely are critical of each other.

* * *

On the wall of the Lambeau Field atrium, among the tiles purchased by fans to help finance the stadium renovation, is one that lists our names and the inscription, "Fans and Friends Forever." We marvel that our friendship and our love for the Packers have lasted fifty years. But of course, we had the best role models. *Jerry Kramer and Fuzzy Thurston, Hornung and McGee.* Lombardi's players were noted for their camaraderie. We lose a couple of our heroes every year now; but the survivors, with few exceptions, remain a close-knit group.

Sometimes we become melancholy because we realize that one year only three of us will be able to make the trip. We are like four differently-shaped pieces of a puzzle; we fit together to form a perfect whole.

BEGINNINGS

"My mom told me, 'Always remember—
It'll spare you a heavy load—
That doctors don't get traded
When their skills get slightly faded,
And dentists don't go on the road.

Have I got a nice guy for ya,
Have a bankah, have a lawyah!'
It's never been clear to me
Why it's OK to play with a CPA
And not with a pro QB."

—Ellen, "Jewish Girls Don't Marry
Quarterbacks," *Third and Long*

GROWING UP (SORT OF) JEWISH IN GREEN BAY

My parents arrived in Green Bay at the end of 1947, fresh from a stint in Florence, Alabama, where the natives not only looked askance at my dad's New York Jewishness, they found him a bit too cordial toward the Negroes in town. To young Sid and Sara, Green Bay must have seemed only slightly more welcoming. Dad made a joke of it, but there must have been some truth:

Around here, when December comes and people put their Christmas trees in the window, everyone gets in their cars and drives around to see the lights. They go like this, "That's a pretty tree ... that's a pretty tree ... oooh, dirty Jew ... hey, that's a pretty tree."

With just a handful of Jewish families in town, only one synagogue was needed, and Congregation Cnesses Israel took the middle ground; it was Conservative. My parents, raised Reform, found the service as foreign as a Catholic Mass and the rabbi uncongenial. They responded by staying home from services, doing their best to assimilate with the Christian population, and rarely talking to me about religion. My dad shortened our last name from Shoenthal—hard to remember, harder to spell—to the more manageable and decidedly less ethnic Shaw.

I didn't find out I was Jewish until I was six, and I was well past my seventh birthday when my parents submitted to peer pressure and reluctantly enrolled me in Sunday school. Only then did I learn that Jews don't celebrate Christmas and Easter. This may tell you where we stood: One year our housekeeper, Frances, took the holiday cards we had received and stood them on the mantelpiece in an attractive arrangement. My mom arrived home from work, saw them, and exclaimed, "Oh no, that looks *goyish!*" So she walked past our own "pretty tree" and took them down.

Naturally, my family didn't keep kosher, but we had our own version of the dietary laws. We gorged on bacon, ham, and the spare ribs made from my dad's prized recipe. But my mother would not allow pork chops or a pork roast in the house. This has given rise to **Linda's Theory of Kosher Devolution.**

Here's how it works:

I'm positive my maternal grandmother, who died before I was born, never let the flesh of swine pass her lips. My mom was more tolerant of pig meat, as long as she wasn't eating something that actually had "pork" in its name. As a twenty-first-century woman and professed atheist, I prepare pork products frequently. However—due to some ingrained fear of trichinosis or damnation—I am compelled to overcook them. Often I bring them to the table gray and dry. So far my son does not cook, but I can predict the day when he, the ultimate product of this reverse evolution, will be confronted with a pork chop and a grill. He will rise to the occasion and offer up a tender, succulent delight.

Speaking of ancestors and food, I have to laugh when I hear the health pronouncement from the whole foods/local foods movement: "Don't eat anything your great-grandmother wouldn't recognize!" *What, you think Great-Grandma knew from EVOO?* I'm sure *my* great-grandmother—at least one of them—cooked everything in artery-clogging chicken fat, rendered by her own hand from a local chicken.

Carla and Del grew up a few blocks away from me in a prestigious development, and to this day they find it hard to believe that my family was not allowed to live there. Del, now a realtor, is blown away by the idea that it would have been her job to steer the Goldfarbs and the Shoenthals to the other side of town! But I remember my mother taking me on walks through that neighborhood. (Whether she took a perverse enjoyment in this, I don't know. I do remember my mother-in-law, years later, declaring that when she died, she hoped to be cremated and have her ashes scattered over another proscribed area, Kenilworth, Illinois.)

I had learned to read at an extremely early age. I recall the neatly-lettered signs with "Sunlight Park" in big, black letters, and I'm positive the tiny print underneath said, "Restricted." Of course, I had no idea what that meant, or that it was accepted practice at the time. As the baby boom flourished, new streets and new houses were constructed all over our suburb of Allouez. When St. Mary's Boulevard was cut through just outside of Sunlight Park, running parallel to St. Francis and Arrowhead Drives, several Jewish families immediately snapped up homes in that favorable location. Among them, the street was referred to as "Cnesses Israel Drive."

How my city-bred father must have wondered at his new world! Next to the tiny starter home my parents bought—and never left—was an older, wooden house where two elderly sisters had turned their entire backyard into a little farm. The plots of flowers and vegetables were separated by miniature boardwalks. In the summer, huge sunflowers hung over the white rail fence between their land and ours. At the back of the sisters' property sat a chicken coop, painted gray to match the house. Agnes and Marie would allow me to toddle after them into its noisy, reeking interior, and my household awakened each morning for years to the crow of their rooster. He soon disabused us of any notion that he would only cock-a-doodle once a day, to herald the dawn!

Other than living outside Sunlight Park, I didn't experience much discrimination. We didn't belong to a country club, but I don't think my parents ever wanted to join one. There was a time when "our kind" was not accepted at the Oneida Golf & Riding Club, but by my teen years, there were several Jewish members and I was always welcome as Pam's guest.

When I asked Pete to a girls-take-boys dance in high school, he first accepted and then called back to say his parents had vetoed the date. But Pete's parents probably wouldn't have let him go with any girl who wasn't Catholic. And fortunately, I wasn't hung up on Pete, although he sure was cute in the blond, crew-cut, All-American mode I favored at the time.

My husband and I have a theory that every Jewish boy, growing up, is attracted to his personal version of the "blonde shiksa goddess," and every

Jewish girl to her "golden goy." Through parents' influence or personal choice,
we may end up with our own kind, but the lure of those others still persists.
The theory may not be sound, but it goes a long way to explain why a certain
P. Hornung so dominated my teenage years.

When I was fourteen and confirmed in a Reform ceremony, I began
to wonder why people I hardly knew were sending me presents and urging
me to become active in B'nai B'rith Youth Organization. Today it's clear.
As the saying goes, it takes a village to raise a Jewish child, and I was
regarded as one in danger of slipping away. I was pushed into attending
a BBYO conclave in Appleton instead of working at a telethon in which
Hornung would be appearing. At the conclave, I was scheduled to present
a chapter scrapbook, which I knew would be a disappointment since I
hadn't bothered to attend any of the BBYO events that I was supposed to
be recording. The stress of impending ridicule over the scrapbook, plus
my yearning for the unattainable Paul, made me literally ill. I grudgingly
attended the conclave with a most unattractive sinus infection.

For some reason, most of the kids my age at Cnesses Israel were female.
There weren't enough boys to go around, but by my senior year in high
school, I'd managed to land one. For purposes of this account, I'll call him
Gabriel. We dated for three years.

At first my folks were glad I was dating a Jewish boy, but they soon
decided he wasn't good enough for me. This part-time college student and
K-Mart floor manager would never become the "professional man" my
parents coveted for their princess. I swear they actively searched for reasons
to dislike him. One time, Gabe had some prior commitment—work or
a family event, something totally legitimate—and was unable to take me
to the East High prom. Since we were "going steady," I couldn't go with
anyone else, and young ladies did not go to the prom unescorted.

It didn't matter how often I told them I didn't care. I'd been to formal
dances before, including one at St. Norbert College with Gabe. In any case,
I was a lousy dancer, and I wasn't close to the people on the prom court.
So missing the event was no cause for tears. But I guess that ever since my
birth, my parents had anticipated sending their little girl off to her senior
prom. They were disappointed, and they blamed him.

Then there was the episode before the senior class party. My parents managed a women's clothing store called Newman's, and once I started to develop an adult figure, they bought most of my clothes there. It was a no-brainer. We got a discount and first dibs on the new styles. But I'd never been asked to "model" anything. I didn't run with the popular social crowd, and no one in school would have chosen attire so they could look like me.

The night of the party, I went into my room to change into clean cutoff jeans and a button-down shirt. That's what all the girls were wearing to this casual affair. However, a new outfit was laid out on my bed. And what an outfit! It had a top made from one of the new synthetic fabrics, printed in harlequin diamonds of bright yellow, hot pink, and black. There was a short, yellow, divided skirt. Below it, shiny tights matched the diamond-printed top. My parents said they'd just received a number of these ensembles at the store, and they'd appreciate it if I'd introduce the style at the party.

Gabe came to pick me up, took one look, and flatly refused to take me anywhere in that getup. I agreed with him—it was awful. My parents were insistent, and finally we gave in. But his reaction gave my parents one more reason to disparage him.

To complicate things, with only one synagogue in town, my relationship with Gabriel was drawing me back into the congregation they'd been shunning. Gabe and I attended a meeting at Cnesses Israel one night while I was in college. I don't remember its purpose, but I became motivated to talk about an experience the two of us had had in Chicago. Scuttling along the sidewalks of the big city, we felt displaced and frightened until we entered a delicatessen filled with familiar smells and faces that looked like the ones around me. People came up to me after the program and hailed this as an epiphany. All would be well, they rejoiced, now that I had discovered my roots. When my mother heard about this—and in a small town, that didn't take long—she was furious.

Then, at the beginning of my sophomore year, Rosh Hashanah came before I had to go back to school, and Gabe had taken off for the holiday. We honestly had nothing better to do, so we decided to attend services. Together. Within minutes after the *shofar* sounded, my mother was once again livid because people were calling to ask her how soon Gabe and I would be married!

Mom had always told me I would go away to college and meet a Nice Jewish Boy. I thought I was in love with Gabriel, but I was open to testing that love. Once I'd arrived at Northwestern University, I even took a class at the Hillel Center on campus, hoping to meet some of those NJBs there. The religion didn't take, and I wasn't getting any dates, so I quit. I found more fertile ground at WNUR, the campus radio station.

But then I discovered that given my Anglicized name, washed-out coloring, and unremarkable nose, the NJBs at the station couldn't tell I was Jewish! I had to advertise by replacing the necklace I'd worn daily for years—a gold football on a chain—with a large Star of David. After a couple of years of mostly-unrequited yearning for the handsome son of a rabbi, I became close to a boy from Chicago's North Shore.

Gabriel, meanwhile, had grown extremely jealous and possessive. I had anticipated going off to Northwestern and bidding him a tearful good-bye. Instead, he followed me to the Chicago area. He moved in with a relative and signed up for classes at a technical college there.

One wintry weekend when we were back in Green Bay, we went to an event at the Brown County Veterans Memorial Arena. As I got out of the car, my heel hit a patch of ice. I went down hard, full-length, on my back and lay still for a moment, stunned. Gabe hurried around the car and leaned over me with an expression of concern. But he didn't ask if I'd been hurt. Instead he urged me, "Hurry! Get up! Your skirt has hiked up, and people are looking at your legs!" The message was clear to me. No one was supposed to see those legs except Gabe.

Gabe also made threats to my new male friends. He went so far as to buy a gun and carve their initials into several bullets. I was almost sure he was bluffing, but no one wanted to take the chance that he wasn't. Eventually two of my best friends at WNUR told me they'd stop seeing me if I didn't cut Gabe loose. It was hard—I still had feelings for him—but I did it.

By this time, the rabbi's son had finished school. That left Scott, the Chicago boy. Here he was, a bona fide NJB—intelligent, creative, bespectacled, overweight, decidedly unathletic, and—*gotta say it—nice.* We graduated from friends to something more, and we were married after I finished school. After years of dreaming about football heroes, it was oddly comfortable to learn that my destiny was something entirely different.

I was lucky to find someone with a Jewish heritage but irreverent views, who would take me as I was. In fact, when my mother decided we had to be married under a canopy and in Chicago, we had to call around to find someone who *knew* a rabbi!

Whatever Mom might have desired, Scott is not a "professional man." He's a successful announcer for broadcast commercials, corporate videos, and the like. In fact, he did the voice tracks for some interactive games located in the Lambeau Field atrium.

As for our son, I guess we were a bad influence. He's an actor and filmmaker. *"My son, the actor." Well, at least he got the last four letters right.*

"I had to advertise by replacing the necklace I'd worn daily for years—a gold football on a chain—with a large Star of David."

See, I did learn something at Cnesses Israel. Funny story about this menorah, though. One December when I was maybe five or six, a package arrived in the mail from my Uncle Dave. It was addressed to me. The holidays were near, so my parents didn't open the package. They saved it and put it under our tree. When I opened it on Christmas morning, the menorah was inside. My folks must have been embarrassed, but it was some time before I found out what my gift really meant. I still have it, and it is the only menorah I have ever owned.

"The tiny starter home my parents bought—and never left"
is dwarfed by the SUV belonging to its present owner.

Courtesy of C. Linda Dowell

Here's a detail from a photo taken in 1962, at Del's fourteenth birthday party.
I'm in back wearing the glasses, and Pam is next to me. Del is in front of us.

HOW WE GOT TOGETHER

At the time we became a unit, I'd known Carla Porter and Dorothy Ellen LeBlanc (who answers only to Del) for most of my life, and Pam Monaghan for a couple of years. But I didn't know any of them very well. Carla and Del were a year behind me in school. Pam was in my grade, but we'd never been in the same homeroom.

Late in 1960, we were on Christmas break from eighth grade when Pam spotted me walking my new puppy, Pauline, past her house. Even though I had the dog (named for guess who), she invited me in. I don't recall whether she was already as silly about the Packers as I was, or whether I made her that way, but this was the beginning of a lifelong friendship that centered on our love for the team.

In spring, when the snow began to melt, there was a new development. Each classroom in our school had been issued one football. The boys had a monopoly on the footballs during the fall quarter, but by spring they had moved on to basketball and baseball. One day at noon recess, as Pam and I strolled across the playground, we saw Carla, Del, and a few other girls capering across the asphalt. We realized they were playing touch football. I had learned to watch sports, but it had never occurred to me that I might actually play football. We came back the next day, and they invited us to join them. We formed teams and played daily for the rest of the school year.

Carla and Del's team, the Grenouilles (French for frogs in the seventh grade vocabulary, but pronounced Wisconsin-style, Gre-*new*-ees) always beat Pam's and mine, aptly dubbed the Doormats. This was partly because the Grenouilles had more talented players and mostly because they cheated shamelessly.

We chose Packer identities and invented nicknames for ourselves. I was "Boydie" for a while, after receiver Boyd Dowler. Pam was "Chickie," because linebacker Dan Currie's name made us think of the chicken curry I had eaten with my grandparents in a New York restaurant. *Don't ask; we were kids.* As our best athlete, Carla had the privilege of being Hornung. At first we gave her the generic nickname of "Swivel Hips," but one day she told us she'd had a dream about kissing Paul and discovering that his lips were sticky. So we modified her name to "Sticky Lips" and merrily chanted: *"Swivel Hips has sticky lips! Sticky Lips has swivel hips!"*

I will never forget the sight of Carla playing quarterback. Her center was a small girl named Margie, who wore a long coat throughout March and April. Margie's coat hung almost to her ankles, making it difficult for her to "hike" the football through her legs. As the little center bent over the ball, Carla would ceremoniously lift the coat and drape it over Margie's upper back. Then a grinning Carla would lift Margie's skirt—yes, we had to wear skirts to school—exposing her underpants, and we would all dissolve in giggles until Margie hastily snapped the ball.

My growing friendship with Carla and Del was special because for me, it represented a step back into childhood. I had matured early and had a woman's figure at age thirteen. Pam was not far behind. We had discovered boys, although they were not yet impressed with us, and we created elaborate fantasies about being the Packers' girlfriends. But Carla and Del were late bloomers and tomboys. Carla, with her hair cut short for summer, resembled a skinny boy, and Del's breastless body mimicked the graceful swoop of a young seal's. Carla and Del were fascinated with my C-cups, and initiated countless games of strip poker, which they manipulated to ensure I would lose. In the middle of one such game, they sent me through Del's second-floor window to retrieve some thrown object, at which point the naughty children closed the window and stranded me on the garage roof in my bra and panties.

Carla and Del instilled in my life a sense of fun that had been missing. Early one summer morning I woke to ratcheting sounds and voices outside my window. The two girls removed the screen and climbed through the open window, landing on top of me in my bed. Another time they informed me that they had an imaginary friend named Quinlan and took me to "Quinlan's house," a circle of bushes that we would have called a "fort" in our younger days. With Pam, we would ride our bikes down to the East River and poke through the reeds, hunting for crayfish. For some reason, we decided that crayfish were Irish and named all the ones we caught "Harrigan."

At thirteen, I had forgotten how to play. Carla and Del pulled me back into a child's world. While Pam's parents and mine were older, sedentary people, Carla and Del had fun-loving, young moms and dads who took ski trips, maintained summer cottages, and encouraged their children to be active. These girls could run and climb, and now I had to keep up with them. I pounded myself into shape on that Allouez School playground. I ached constantly, but it was a satisfying ache, a mark of accomplishment. For the first time, I experienced the rhythm of my feet hitting the ground, my body connected at the core, all the muscles working together. As I toil today in fitness classes full of aging baby boomers, I still feel that sweet connection from time to time, and I always think of Carla when I do.

Del was a friend, and over the years she has become a better friend, but in those early days, it was Carla who was the attraction for me. I found her nothing short of magical. When our parents were around, she seemed quiet and mousy, but when it was just us kids, this little sprite became Carla the Bold, Carla the Magnificent, the ringleader of all our activities. It was Carla's soft lips I practiced kissing long before any boy cared to try, and it was Carla for whom I felt a pang of jealousy when she finally claimed her first boyfriend—and suddenly became, for me, like all the other girls. To Del's credit, although she and Carla had been friends long before I came into the picture, she never made me feel that I had come between her and Carla.

I was nerdy enough that I wrote poems to Carla several times during our high school years. I don't remember showing them to her then, but I sent her copies, with a wry note, when I discovered my scribblings years later. Some excerpts:

What is this that you ask me to do?
To mock Maturity?
To scorn Society?
To force Convention to let down her hair?
Am I to leap the barriers of Time
And run again through the fields like a wild thing?
Seek your folly somewhere else.
You come too late to me.

* * *

When did I lose you?
The day I saw you fall in love
Perhaps the thousandth time, and saw that love
Returned ... the first.
The day that all that elfin, virgin promise
Turned to woman's cheaper glory ...

I can hardly believe that impassioned, teenage voice was mine.

Courtesy of C. Linda Dowell

Carla at sixteen.

BELONGING

My three friends and the Packers gave me something to belong to. As early as I can remember, I felt like an outsider. When I was very small, there were no other children within walking distance of my home. The front of my house faced busy Webster Avenue, and in back there was nothing for a mile but a vast sweep of weeds that resembled miniature grain stalks, all the way down to the East River. A precocious reader, I passed my days with books and paper dolls.

I was four when my mother went to work at the store with my father. They hired an older, single woman named Frances as our housekeeper. Fran had been a teacher, but I heard my folks whisper that she'd had a "nervous breakdown" and could no longer control a class. Cleaning a little house and caring for one child—those were tasks she could handle. Our dining room/library was converted to a bedroom for Fran, and she shared our single bathroom. I always found it ironic that our house was smaller than any I visited, yet we were the family that had live-in help.

Frances and I came to love each other during the seventeen years she spent with us, but she rarely played with me. In those days my elders believed that excessive use of the eyes could permanently harm a child's vision, as if I could actually use up my ability to see. *These are the same people who told me a few years later that I'd get sick if I washed my hair more than once a week.* So for a couple of hours after lunch each day, I was torn away from my books and drawings and sent out to the backyard. Since I didn't have anyone to play with and I hated getting dirty, I spent most of that time sitting on the steps and cringing each time an insect crawled or flew by. I couldn't wait to be allowed back in so I could huddle by the big console radio and listen to the afternoon kids' shows. There was no chance I'd ruin my eyes watching TV. Green Bay didn't have a station until 1952, and then it was a while before we bought a set.

I did have some playmates, but I saw them mainly on weekends when my parents were around to provide transportation or to supervise us. My dad found a kindred spirit in Russ Widoe, who in time became a local television personality. My first friend was his daughter Judy. Their big, spooky, Victorian house featured a turret and was filled with Russ's collection of Asian art. This exotic abode was a perfect place to act out the mysteries and ghost stories that Judy and I both loved. We fashioned costumes from fabrics gleaned from my grandfather's import business. Our talismans were glow-in-the-dark skull charms that we'd been lucky enough to capture from gum machines.

And my parents became friendly with a couple named Bob and Marcia Deutsch, Hanukkah-bush Jews like us, who eventually had six children. *("We're not Catholic, we're just careless!" Bob would joke.)* Bob was the president of Schreiber's Cheese, and for years he tried unsuccessfully to get my dad interested in trying exotic cheeses. Believe it or not, I grew up in Wisconsin and we never had anything in the house but packaged American and Swiss.

The two oldest Deutsch children were girls. Robin was a year younger than I, and Mady two years younger. I was sometimes allowed to tag along with the Deutsches on their outings, and they gave me a taste of normal family life in those times. I remember that they introduced me to my first milkshake, at a restaurant on Riverside Drive called The Shrimp Shack. When poodle skirts became popular, Marcia sewed one for me from bright blue felt, carefully affixing three-dimensional pom-poms to the poodle's appliquéd body. And I learned from the Deutsches that when you cheered, you yelled, "yay," not "hurrah" like the children in my dusty books.

In time the baby boom came to full fruition, and the weeds were mowed down to make room for sprawling ranch houses and streets where children played. Judy and I spent our Sunday afternoons for years exploring, climbing, and—inspired by Nancy Drew—looking for "clues" in the half-finished homes. But when the new neighbors arrived, I was awkward and shy with them.

I'm sure my primary-grade teachers often shook their heads over me. When I started school, I could read chapter books, but my social skills were nonexistent. When I didn't feel comfortable, I slapped my classmates or pulled their hair. I ran clumsily with my arms at my sides, because no one had taught me to pump them. And because my parents had always told me I was supposed to be the brightest and the best, I cried each time I got even one answer wrong on a test. All of this naturally made me a target of ridicule. I knew a lot from books, but I didn't know how to be a kid.

The boys, of course, wanted nothing to do with me. I eventually found my place among the girls, with whom I shared activities such as Girl Scouts and piano lessons.

My friendship with Pam, Carla, and Del happened at just the right time. By seventh grade, my status had again begun to change. My classmates were putting away dolls and toys and having boy-girl parties. When Judy had a party and didn't invite me, I was dejected, especially when our homeroom teacher, young Mr. Zweck, joked with the kids about some kissing that had taken place at the party. I think my parents must have said something to Judy's, because I was invited to her next party. But as she had anticipated, I didn't fit in. To make things worse, a certain blond, crew-cut classmate—the first-ever "golden *goy*" on my radar—professed his affection for Judy, not me.

Being Jewish contributed to my feeling that I played by different rules. It seemed to me that Jewish parents, or mine at least, put a different emphasis on child rearing than Gentile ones did. For one thing, the *goyish* parents spent their money in other ways. They took vacations with and without their children; my parents hardly ever took a vacation, but worked so that I could go to camp all summer. My hometown friends, who occasionally managed a week or two at Scout camp, couldn't understand why I went to a private camp for eight weeks every summer. But my New York–raised dad had done that before me, and most of my fellow campers were Jewish girls from the Chicago suburbs.

And it seemed to me the Gentile parents raised their children to face risks, while the Jewish ones were likely to be overprotective. My folks were still hiring a babysitter for me when I was twelve and other girls my age were earning money by sitting.

For years, I aspired to be just like everybody else. Because my paternal grandfather was an importer, he and my grandmother traveled frequently to Europe. The party clothes they sent back for me included smart, miniature navy blue suits and embroidered smocks. I'd probably consider them "to die for" if I had a granddaughter to dress up today. But when I was little, I wanted pink or yellow ruffled dresses like the ones my classmates got from the local department stores. Years later, when my son coveted some ridiculously expensive athletic shoes, I remembered those party dresses. The kid got his shoes.

Since my parents hailed from outside the state—Dad from New York, and Mom from Russia by way of Indiana—we didn't even talk like Green Bay people. For example, in that part of the country, a drinking fountain is generally called a "bubbler." I finally got used to saying "bubbler" when I was about eighteen and left for college, where of course, nobody knew what I meant.

Although my family didn't have roots in Green Bay, my convivial father quickly found a niche. But I'm not sure my mother ever was happy there. She had grown up in Fort Wayne, Indiana—in no way a metropolis, but still a city about three times the size of Green Bay, with a larger Jewish population. She considered Green Bay a backwater, and made fun of the local argot. At that time, many of the older people—country people, likely of Belgian heritage, as so many were—had a habit of finishing declarative sentences with a lilting "and so," much as Canadians might conclude with "eh." *"Enso, enso?"* my mother would imitate them, screwing up her face.

Mom taught me that for special purchases, quality purchases, one didn't shop in Green Bay but looked to New York, Chicago, or at the very least, Milwaukee. It struck me as hilarious when I spent a summer in Door County, Wisconsin, and learned that people there considered Green Bay their shopping mecca. (I chuckled in delighted recognition years later when I heard a number by Da Yoopers. That comic troupe sang about women from Michigan's Upper Peninsula, sneaking off to Green Bay to shop while their husbands are hunting deer.)

I suppose that because I didn't fit in, I needed heroes more than the next child. I developed huge crushes on the Packers, camp counselors—even, in a sense, Carla. I craved role models, and I wasn't finding them at home.

My mother might have been more comfortable in my generation than she was in her own. Late in her career, she complained about her role at Newman's. She claimed that she did all the hard work, while my dad was out *schmoozing* and claiming whatever credit was due for the store's success. This may have been true, since she was the one who came home several weekends each year with huge ledgers and spent hours updating them.

As I saw it, she had no life. My parents would play cards or go to parties as a couple, with my father's friends and their wives. But my mother had no genuine girlfriends, no one with whom she chatted on the phone, tried out new looks, or shared hobbies. She often came home from the store too tired even to bathe—yet not too tired to throw back a few measures of Scotch. There was almost nothing of her left for my father, and it was he with whom I privately sided when his attentions began to stray.

Of course, Mom's job kept her from sharing most of my activities. I remember one occasion when she tried. When I was in grade school, my Girl Scout troop spent several meetings after school learning to bowl at the Kegler's Klub, a few blocks south of my home near the Allouez–De Pere line. At the end we held a mother-daughter bowling party. To my surprise, my mother appeared. She rolled what might have been her first line ever, still in her work outfit of knitted dress and matching jacket, her slim, nylon-clad legs disappearing into the clunky, multicolored, rented shoes. I think she scored seventeen. At the time, I was embarrassed, comparing her with the other moms and wishing she hadn't bothered to come. Today I appreciate what she did.

After I left early childhood, I barely accepted my mother. I knew she loved me; but, unfair as it was, I found her love cloying, overly sentimental, and frankly, inconvenient. If she had lived more than fifteen months past the day I made her a grandmother, I think we might have found more common ground. But she died in 1979 at age sixty-three, a victim of cardiac disease brought on by chain-smoking. I was not among the eulogists at her funeral. I sat in wonder as mourners spoke of an astute, capable businesswoman; a person I had never known.

The Packers had made me love my hometown. But I always felt that I was being groomed to leave, and to me that seemed tragic. After dark I could look from my bedroom window across the river to the stadium, where eight lights high on stanchions alerted airplanes that the field was there. Seeing those lights, I felt secure.

I was proud to be a Wisconsinite. Braving the long winters made me feel tough and superior. And when moisture came through the porous walls of our stucco house and formed frost on my bedroom walls—yes, on the inside—it seemed romantic, like something Jane Eyre or Laura Ingalls Wilder might have endured. When I grew up and moved south, my surroundings always seemed too lush. Cleaning my house near Washington, DC, I was dismayed to find that what I'd thought for weeks was a wire for a stereo speaker was actually a vine. It had insinuated itself under a crack in the siding and sprouted into my living room where it was flourishing behind the media bench. What I'd taken for dust on the wire—the impetus for my cleaning—was a resident colony of tiny insects. My first indignant reaction was, "This would never happen in Wisconsin!"

I loved Green Bay's gently rolling terrain, with a few modest hills to the east of the city. Scray's Hill was the one where the teenagers went to "park." We could look down from the top and see the lights of the city spread below. Most of the radio and TV towers were up there. We had three AM radio stations in those days—FM wasn't a big deal yet—and for some reason they'd been crowded onto frequencies 1360, 1400, and 1440. Sit up there on Scray's, tune in for some mood music, and sometimes we could hear all three of them at once. While I was dating Gabriel, he purchased a Dodge Charger with a huge engine, an eight-track player (think giant cassettes) and seats that folded down in the back *so we could, um, carry large pieces of cargo.* We'd take it up the hill when we were in town. I think he felt like James Bond in that car.

I could envision myself married to Gabe, living in a little apartment, working for the *Press-Gazette* newspaper or one of the broadcast stations, and, of course, attending all the Packer games. I'd get my name in the paper; people around town would recognize me. I'd have my place. But I knew that wasn't my parents' dream for me.

I finally fulfilled their expectations by marrying my North Shore NJB and moving away. Although Newman's had an extensive bridal department, there was no question of outfitting me there. Instead, my mother took a rare day off to shepherd me and Pam around Chicago, where we eventually found a dress at Marshall Field's.

And yet, after more than forty years of living somewhere else, I still call Green Bay my home and the Packers my team. As a Packer fan, I do belong to something. I can walk around anywhere in the country wearing the green and gold, and perfect strangers will stop me to talk about their uncle in Oshkosh or their brother who loves the Pack.

And Pam, Del, and Carla continue to be among my closest friends. They made a place in their lives for an awkward, fearful child. They accepted her, supported her, and helped her to grow. And they still do.

HALCYON

"Hell of a world where being a winner
Means we don't get to enjoy our dinner.
Livin' in a fishbowl here ...
Where can we hide, when we're so sizable?
Football stars are recognizable.
Livin' in a fishbowl, in a fishbowl ..."

—John and Rick, "Livin' in a Fishbowl,"
Third and Long

DOWNTOWN WAS
OUR PLAYGROUND

Memories fade, but I'll do my best to reconstruct downtown Green Bay as I remember it in the fifties and sixties. First, let's make sure you can locate it. Wisconsin, as you learned in your grade-school geography class, is shaped like a mitten—although not as expertly knitted as its mate Michigan, next door. The space between the thumb and the fingers is Green Bay, the bay. Green Bay, the city, is located at the juncture, and the Fox River trails down from there like an errant piece of yarn.

The river divided the city, but most of downtown was on the East Side. The main thoroughfare was Washington Street, which ran parallel to, and just east of, the river. It had the usual collection of square buildings, two or three stories in height, some with taller false fronts in the style of the previous century. The north-south streets were named for presidents—Washington, Adams, and so on—and most of the east-west streets were named for trees. There was indeed a Main Street, but it was almost an afterthought, running parallel to the tree streets at the north end of town. Three bridges spanned the Fox: at Mason, just south of downtown; at Walnut; and at Main. Looking up Washington Street toward Main, the world appeared to drop off abruptly just past the Hurlbut Coal Company clock, where the river ran out to the bay.

My parents' store, Newman's, was on Washington, between Walnut and Cherry Streets. It was part of a subsidiary chain of the Lane Bryant

Company, and it sold women's clothing in all sizes, not just the plus sizes associated with Lane Bryant. A corner of the drafty, unfinished third floor had been partitioned off and made into a cozy office for my father and his secretary. My dad had aspired to become a professional actor—"Shaw" was originally intended to be his stage name—but when he landed a secure job during the Great Depression, he elected to play it safe. He was active for years, though, in the Green Bay Community Theater. He lined the walls of his office with stills from CT productions and shelves of printed scripts from the Fireside Theater book club. I'd come downtown after school, curl up on his rickety couch with one of those books, and immerse myself in the latest Broadway hit.

Next door to Newman's was a big sporting goods store, Bertrand's. I bought my first football there, at age thirteen, for three dollars. Across the street was Nau's, another women's store and the main competition for Newman's. The H.C. Prange Company, two blocks down Washington between Pine and Main, was our town's major department store. Prange's restaurant, the Terrace Room, was the preferred site for little girls' birthday parties. They provided each birthday girl with a special cake, baked in a bowl and inverted. Into the resulting half-sphere was inserted, to the waist, a doll. The cake became her skirt, and decorative frosting was used on the doll's torso and the cake to create an elegant ball gown worthy of any Disney princess.

Prange's had a beauty salon, and starting when I was eleven or twelve, my mother made fortnightly appointments for me to have my hair washed and styled there. In those days, women of a certain age and class made regular appointments to have their hair teased, sculpted, and permed into elaborate 'dos, and woe betide them if anything happened to those hairdos between appointments, because they professed to be powerless to do anything about it. After I was married, my mother-in-law would come to visit bearing her own satin-covered bed pillow, the better to protect her curls.

My home's single bathroom had only a tub with no shower, and by the time I was eleven or so, I resisted my mother's attempts to wash my hair with a spray attachment pushed onto the faucet of the little sink. But my solo efforts invariably resulted in a flooded bathroom. My mother's solution was Prange's salon. I'd go every other Saturday—Mom thought that was quite often enough to wash a girl's hair—for a shampoo and set, plus a manicure. Then I'd have lunch at the counter of Prange's casual restaurant, the Pine Room. The manicurist's oil would mingle with the greasy juices from my cheeseburger, coating my fingers with a singular slickness and aroma.

Eventually my parents installed a shower over the tub, and my salon dates were over except for occasional haircuts. However, I did make a special trip in the fall of 1962, when I was cast in East High's sophomore-junior play, *Time Out for Ginger*. Pam and I had already read and loved Ronald Alexander's play, in which a girl tries out for her high school football team, and I thought it was fate when auditions were announced. Alas, the part of Ginger went to a petite junior named Janet. She got the honor of dressing up in a jersey and shoulder pads and posing for the cover of a fake *Life* magazine. But I was cast as Ginger's mother, Agnes. To look the part, I went to Prange's and had my hair styled and coated with a thick, gray spray. I came in late from the cast party Saturday night, slept in, and got up just in time to go to the Packer game on Sunday. The house was full of guests after the game, so I didn't shower then. My hair was still gray when we headed out for dinner at the Spot supper club. I hoped we'd meet some Packers and they'd comment on my new adult look. Indeed, we ran into Boyd Dowler and his wife. I was gratified by Boyd's asking, "What *is* that?" although I had to fluff my hair several times before he noticed it.

We had three movie theaters: the Bay on Washington Street; the Orpheum, later the Vic, on Walnut; and the West, across the Walnut Street bridge from downtown. The Bay and Vic showed the latest features, while the West had the long-running blockbusters and a sprinkling of art films. All were good places to keep cool in the summer, since most homes in that time and climate did not have air conditioning.

The Kellogg Public Library on Jefferson Street was an ideal place to feed my growing interest in sports. There I learned to admire the classic reporting of Grantland Rice, who coined the nickname of Notre Dame's Four Horsemen; and Red Smith, a graduate of Green Bay East High School. When I expanded my interests to include baseball, I found delightful short stories by Ring Lardner, and Mark Harris's wonderful Henry Wiggen series. Also there for the taking were the sports novels of John R. Tunis, written for kids my age but already slightly outdated and sweetly nostalgic.

The Camera Corner moved, sometime during the sixties, from the southeast corner of Washington and Walnut to the northwest corner. It was owned by a neighbor of ours and my parents' good friend, Norman Chernick. Norm's son Rick—my playmate Caryn's little brother Ricky—came into the business when he grew up. He added video equipment, then jumped on the IT bandwagon and grew the business far beyond the humble camera store. Today, like many successful local businessmen, he sits on the Packers' board of directors. *Now there's an NJB my mama might have approved!*

My friends and I frequented three dime stores on Washington Street— genuine five-and-tens that sold toys, candy, junk jewelry, comic books, craft materials, small pets, forty-five RPM records, and the other little things our allowances would cover. They were the H.L. Green Company, Woolworth's, and Kresge's, which I think is the one where Del and Carla once shoplifted a big block of chocolate. *(What? It's been fifty years!)* Woolworth's was the biggest, with a good-sized lunch counter. When I read about sit-ins at lunch counters in Southern states, I always pictured them at that counter. However, there was little chance of our local Woolworth's refusing service to Packer stars like Willie Davis and Willie Wood, the only "Negroes" I knew!

There was an Osco chain pharmacy and two smaller drugstores, which also had lunch counters and tables. My parents often took their meal breaks at Charley Brock's drugstore on Walnut Street, owned by a Packer player from the forties. One day my father spotted Lew Carpenter, a current Packer running back, and invited him to join the three of us there. Carpenter's foot fell asleep while he sat with us, so when he rose from the table, he limped noticeably. Lew joked—not without reason—that by nightfall the entire town would be gossiping that he had been put on injured reserve.

Across Walnut Street from Brock's drugstore were two other establishments of note. A bar called The Office was a popular hangout, not for the Packers, but for the Green Bay Bobcats hockey team. Dad told me he was there one night when it appeared that a fight would break out. As the tension built, he saw a half dozen hockey players prudently removing their false front teeth and putting them into their pockets!

A couple of doors down from The Office was the original home of Sammy's Pizza. (The current location is on the West Side near the stadium.) I tasted pizza for the first time when I was eleven. My parents' store closed at five o'clock most days, but on Friday nights it was open until nine, and my folks would often come home with some sort of carry-out dinner. One night my dad bore a flat, greasy package that smelled like nothing I'd ever encountered before. He, of course, was familiar with pizza from his New York days, but it was new to Green Bay. Dad had selected a kosher salami topping, assuming that my mother would not eat pepperoni or sausage. The salami became our staple. There is a certain style of pizza that I've never found anywhere but the upper Midwest—light on the tomato sauce, heavy on cheese and oregano, with a thin, crispy, cracker-like crust. To me—and, I think, to Pam—it is still the gold standard of pizza.

The second small drugstore/luncheonette, at the north end of Washington Street, was John Holzer's. This little store was always overheated, redolent of cooking grease, and lined with peeling, yellowing clippings from the sports pages. This was supposed to be a good place to spot Packer players, but I never saw one there. It always amazed me that the Packers attracted "super-fans" who became local celebrities in their own right and earned mentions in the *Press-Gazette*. Holzer was one of these. Another was Paul Mazzoleni, who owned a gas station and car wash on the West Side and washed the Packers' cars for free. (Mazzoleni is now a member of the Packers FAN Hall of Fame.) And a third was Howie Blindauer, who haunted the practice field during training camp, passing out rosters imprinted with ads for his sheet-metal business.

In the future we would meet costumed characters—including St. Vince, who appears at games in a bishop's miter emblazoned with an image of Lombardi; and the Packalope, who wears a buck's antlers attached to a vintage Packer helmet. But during the sixties, the super-fans were simply local businessmen who were recognized for their extreme devotion to the team.

The jewel of Washington Street was a wonderland called Kaap's. Owned by an elderly German couple, Kaap's was a combination candy store, bakery, restaurant, and bar. When we came through the main entrance, we were in the candy and baked-goods section, surrounded by high glass cases and the most wonderful smells. In the cases were heavily-enrobed chocolates, the sugary mint wafers that became a staple on party tables, buttery caramels, tall cakes, puffy fruit-filled pastries called *kolaches*, almond crescents, and more. But not all of the delights were inside the cases. Above them were displayed intricately carved cuckoo clocks, wooden toy villages, and a large selection of expensive stuffed animals by Steiff. The rooms beyond the bakery were lined with tall, dark, shiny, wooden booths and lamps that resembled carriage lamps. We could get a hamburger, a sandwich, or a complete dinner for a reasonable price, and finish with ice cream and hot fudge sauce made in-house. The bar featured every cocktail that had been invented, listed on a card in alphabetical order. My dad had a friend who was trying to drink his way through that alphabetical list, though I doubt he ever made it!

Kaap's, just a block from my parents' store, was the first restaurant Judy and I were allowed to enter alone. When we were ten or eleven, we could take a Saturday morning art class at the Neville Public Museum next to the library on Jefferson Street, walk three blocks to Newman's to check in, and on down to Kaap's for our lunch. I'm still friendly with Judy, who now lives in Door County, Wisconsin, and a few years ago she gave me a framed print of the façade of Kaap's. It has a place of honor on my dining room wall.

Green Bay was a typical, medium-sized, Midwestern business center of its time, with papermaking and cheese manufacturing as its main industries—except for one big difference. For me, Pam, Carla, and Del, downtown became our playground and our Packer hunting ground. One particular corner, at Adams and Pine Streets, became known to Pam and me as Normie–Johnny–Willie–Herbie Corner, because we spotted Packer players Norm Masters, John Roach, Willie Davis, and Herb Adderley on that corner on separate occasions.

The Northland Hotel, Green Bay's largest, sat at the corner of Adams and Pine. One day all four of us were downtown together, and as we passed it we noticed Curly Lambeau, the Packers' founder and longtime coach, going in with some other men. We peeked in and watched the group enter the hotel restaurant and settle at a table by the window. So we pressed our noses against that window and made faces at the legendary Curly Lambeau. *(There really* wasn't *much to do in Green Bay when the Packers weren't playing!)*

The Packers' opponents stayed at the Northland. One Saturday afternoon before a game with the Baltimore Colts, our quartet spotted their star halfback Tom Matte exiting the hotel. Much to his annoyance, we marched behind him for several blocks. Finally he turned and asked us just what we thought we were doing. Ever honest and loyal, we replied, "Trying to make you nervous so you won't play well tomorrow!" When Matte committed a costly fumble in Sunday's game, we knew we had acquitted ourselves well.

And it was just down Pine Street from the famous corner that we spotted Paul Hornung and defensive end Bill Quinlan on December 23, 1961. We hadn't expected Hornung, since this was the year of the Berlin crisis, when a number of NFL players, including Paul, were called up to their military reserve units. Hornung was stationed with the Army at Fort Riley, Kansas, and each week the fans were on tenterhooks as we waited to hear if he would get a weekend pass to play in Sunday's game. Legend has it Lombardi actually called President Kennedy to make sure Paul got his pass for the NFL championship game against the New York Giants. This game was still more than a week away, so we greeted Paul with delight and congratulated him on his early release. As he and Quinlan walked away, it hit me. Today was Paul's twenty-sixth birthday. I'd had the chance to wish my favorite player a happy birthday, and I'd blown it. "Let's follow him!" Del and Carla urged.

So we trailed Paul on his errands. Like Matte, he soon caught on and was less than pleased. But we finally cornered him at a counter in Prange's where he was waiting for his purchase to be bagged. "Mr. Hornung," I pleaded. He turned, glowering. Quickly I blurted, "I just wanted to wish you a happy birthday!"

Paul's face smoothed out, and he smiled. "Aw, Paul," Quinlan growled, "give the young lady a hug!" His huge arm swung out and smashed me into Paul's stomach. I could hardly breathe as I felt Paul's arms wrapping around me. I felt a disturbing mix of chagrin and elation.

There were other magical places for me in downtown Green Bay. The Packer ticket and corporate offices were located on South Washington Street until they moved out to the stadium later in the sixties. I loved the glass display windows of the ticket office, filled with photos of every team since the Packers' inception in 1919. I could stand in front of those windows for hours, marveling at the leather helmets and memorizing the names and faces of Don Hutson, Johnny Blood, Arnie Herber, and their likes. Although current players rarely appeared there, the ticket office was a regular stop on my rounds.

When we became old enough to drive, we'd occasionally cruise by restaurants and taverns that the Packers were known to patronize. One night during our senior year in high school, Pam had brought along a little East De Pere freshman and we were *(groan!)* training her in the art of Packer-hunting, presumably to preserve our legacy when we went off to college. We pulled up at the curb across Monroe Street from a bar called Speed's. "Is this where Paul Hornung goes?" the young girl asked in awe.

"He might," Pam answered, "but don't believe everything you hear. People say a lot of things about him that aren't true." At that very moment, the door of Speed's opened, and the great man walked out.

I've referred more than once to the gossip about Hornung, so I guess I should give you an illustration. He was often referred to as "Piccadilly Paul," after another club he frequented. The story was that he had performed a strip-tease at the Piccadilly. His version—probably a lot more accurate— was that while relaxing there, he had removed his sport coat and opened his shirt. But rumors grow exponentially in a small town.

Hornung was regarded as the league's most eligible bachelor until "Broadway Joe" Namath came along in the late sixties to steal the title. As Paul reported in his own book, *Golden Boy* (see reference page at the end of this book), he arrived at his first Packers' training camp to find a girl waiting for him. A friend had posed as Paul and written to invite her. Later that season, an injured Hornung was sitting on the bench during a game in Los Angeles. A young lady came down onto the field and wouldn't leave until Paul posed for a picture with her.

I don't want to give you the impression that Hornung, or any Packers of that time, had an agenda of sleeping with all the local lovelies. If someone's behavior had become an embarrassment to the team, I'm sure Lombardi would have shipped the offender right out of Green Bay. Still, these were healthy young men, and stuff happened sometimes. Carla got an interesting phone call a couple of years ago from an adoptee looking for her birth parents. This young woman had learned that her father was a Packer in the sixties—*no, not Paul*—and her mother was a girl about our age who, like Del and Carla, had lived on Arrowhead Drive. The daughter had found Carla through the Internet. None of us recognized her mom's name, though. She must not have gone to the public schools.

By my college years, I'd discovered Art's Tailor Shop on Cherry Street, next to Bosse's News Depot. Art was a small, Jewish man who had a daughter around my age. He did custom tailoring, and the Packers had adopted him as a source for large-sized clothing that couldn't be found in the local stores. Art was kind enough to relate to me the latest team gossip as I hung out in hopes that one of his oversized clients would pass through the door. I remember having a conversation with tight end Marv Fleming there. I informed him that he resembled a boy I liked at college, except that guy was Jewish while Marvin was African American. Marv made some remark about the Lost Tribes, apparently oblivious that I was saying I found him attractive.

That downtown is a dim memory. In the late seventies the town fathers implemented a new concept in an effort to compete with suburban shopping centers. They collected most of the stores into a downtown shopping plaza, turning the streets into a pedestrian mall. The concept failed; suburban sprawl still rules, and the big plaza is now closed. The only buildings we recognized on a recent trip were the Bay Theater (now the Meyer Theater, which hosts live productions) and the Bellin Building at the corner of Washington and Walnut, where I used to visit my eye doctor.

For a while, the ticket office became a bar called The Glory Years, attached to the Best Western Motel—which I remember as the Downtowner, the first motel in Green Bay to feature an indoor swimming pool. When we visited the bar in 1998, we were surprised to find, inside the ladies' room, a large poster of Hornung, liberally adorned with lipstick "smooches." My friends and I posed before it, throwing kisses to the young Paul.

Courtesy of C. Linda Dowell

The Miss Wisconsin float from the dedication parade for new City Stadium (later Lambeau Field) in 1957. My parents' store may have helped to dress some of these lovely ladies.

"The world appeared to drop off abruptly just past the Hurlbut Coal Company clock, where the river ran out to the bay." Next to the clock was the Spot supper club, frequented by Packer players, coaches, and my family.

Courtesy of the Neville Public Museum of Brown County

Washington Street in the 1960s. This is one block north of my parents' store, Newman's. Kaap's, in the middle of the block, was the first restaurant my friend Judy and I were allowed to enter alone.

Press-Gazette Collection of the Neville Public Museum of Brown County

Interior of Kaap's. "The rooms beyond the bakery were lined with tall, dark, shiny, wooden booths and lamps that resembled carriage lamps."

RAILBIRDS

My girlfriends and I loved to watch the Packers practice, but before we could drive, it wasn't easy to get to their field. Today there's a bridge in Allouez, a quick hop to the stadium complex and airport, but back then we had to make a long circuit through downtown Green Bay. From Allouez we took the East De Pere bus, which ran only once an hour. It took thirty minutes or more to get downtown, and then we transferred to the Ninth Street bus, which took us over the Fox River to the West Side. Getting off at Ninth and Oneida, we still had several blocks to walk, so the trip took about an hour.

One chilly morning when we had a school holiday, the four of us made the trek, only to find that Coach Lombardi had moved practice inside the stadium. We circled the huge oval, hoping to find a gap in its chain-link fence. Then we came upon a gate that inexplicably was raised more than a foot above the ground. I couldn't resist. The kid who hated to get dirty dropped to the pavement. I rolled, squeezed, and wriggled, and finally found myself on the other side—staring at a large pair of feet. A tall man with a gray crew cut was looking down at me. It was Tom Miller, a former player and now the Packers' business manager. Despite our protestations that he knew all of our fathers and we were not there to sell secrets to the Chicago Bears, he would not let us stay, so we made the long return trip unfulfilled.

Each summer day starting in mid-July, several hundred people would line the bleachers along the practice field, across Oneida Street from the stadium. There was only one field then, in contrast to the large indoor/outdoor complex located there today. I remember waiting on those bleachers for the team to come down from the locker room. The sideline would be quiet—a few cars going past, a few insects humming—and then suddenly the air would explode with outlandish sounds—the clumping of cleats, loud grunts like seals barking, singing, shouting of nicknames. *(Trees! Dapper! Dapperdappadappadappa ...)* And then the players would come down to us, leaving cleat marks like exotic animal tracks and seeming an entirely different species from the rest of us.

By the time I reached my mid-teens, it took me longer to get ready for Packer practice than it did for my dates with high-school boys. After all, whom did I want to impress more? I'd tease my hair on top, coax the ends to flip up evenly all around, and anchor the 'do with a blast of Aqua-Net. Next would come a little eye makeup—enough to show behind my glasses, but not enough to run if the day got warm. Thanks to my new interest in physical exercise, my stomach was finally flat. I'd smooth my cutoff jeans over my belly and roll them neatly above my well-shaved knees.

When I was in my early teens, my figure was definitely *zaftig*. "Hippy" was my grandmother's word, and she wasn't talking about pot smoking or communes. I eventually honed my body into some semblance of a teen queen's through numerous sit-ups and squat-thrusts. Today women do crunches instead of sit-ups, and I think squat-thrusts are extinct, condemned as knee- and back-killers. They were just what they sound like: Drop into a frog position, kick your legs out behind you, then pull them back in and stand up. They might have been dangerous, but I'd watched the Packers do them in practice, so whenever I performed them, I felt empowered.

Of course, we often saw the Packers' wives on the practice-field sidelines. We greeted them and admired their children. *"Aw, he looks just like his daddy. And check out the size of those hands. I bet he can grip a football already."* But oddly, for all of Pam's and my aspirations, we never tried to make friends or mentors of them. Like their husbands, they seemed to us exotic creatures. Many of the wives were Southern girls, and in public at least, they displayed the poise and gleaming smiles of the cheerleaders and homecoming queens they had been. At fifteen or sixteen, we felt big and clumsy beside their petite perfection. We should have asked for referrals to a fairy godmother!

My father took me to the practice field on what proved to be a historic occasion. There was a tower on the field, about twenty-five feet tall. It allowed coaches to see formations from a different angle and also could be used for filming. That day a squall of wind and rain sprang up, and suddenly there was a commotion on the field. I couldn't see what had happened, but the tower was gone, and all the players were running to where it had been. Practice eventually resumed, and it was only that night when the *Press-Gazette* came out (a morning paper now but an evening paper then) that I learned the tower had fallen over on Ray Nitschke. Ray had gone over to the base of the tower to get his helmet, to protect his balding head from the rain. Fortunately he had already put it on when the wind blew the tower down, because a bolt from the structure pierced the helmet and went almost all the way through it. That helmet is now on display in the Packers Hall of Fame. Ray, perhaps the quintessential middle linebacker, didn't need anything to enhance his reputation of toughness, but this incident surely did.

Shortly before we got our driver's licenses, Pam and I prevailed upon an older girl—I'll call her Lisa—to chauffeur us to some of the practices. Pam and I thought redheaded Lisa would attract the players' attention, and this worked well both for us and for her.

Lisa snagged a few dates with a guard named Ed Blaine. When she told me Ed enjoyed the music of the New Christy Minstrels, I immediately bought a Christies' album and remained their fan for years. Lisa also mentioned that the amiable Ed intended to go to medical school. "I bet he'll have a wonderful bedside manner," I enthused—shocking myself more than Lisa with my unplanned *double entendre*.

Blaine was traded to the Philadelphia Eagles, and Lisa started seeing another handsome bachelor who had joined the Packers. She reported to Pam and me one day that her new friend had caramel-colored sheets on his bed. This impressed me, but not the way she'd expected. Our conversation might have gone something like this:

Me: Caramel-*colored?*
Lisa: Yeah, caramel. And he's such a great kisser …
Me: I've never seen caramel-colored sheets.
Lisa: The bottom sheet was the solid color, and the top sheet had caramel-and-white stripes. Mmm, he's so good-looking and so different from the guys around here.
Me: My mom only ever buys white ones, or really blah pale pink or yellow.
Lisa: I'm going to see him again on Thursday.
Me: Some day I'm *going to have caramel-colored sheets …*

My horizons were expanding. Soon I would leave the pallid pastels of my childhood bedroom and go out into the world, where in due time I would embrace the brilliant patterns of Vera and Marimekko. I have always purchased vividly-colored sheets for my own home, and I still think of Lisa's "Packer man," with his roguish grin and unruly mop of hair, when I make up my beds.

Quarterback Bart Starr works out on the Oneida
Street practice field during the 1960s.

Part of the Packers' indoor practice facility, as it looks today.

Henry Lefebvre Collection of the Neville Public Museum of Brown County

Inside the Packers' locker room during Lombardi's tenure. From left to right, Vince Lombardi, Jim Ringo, Boyd Dowler, Ron Kramer, Jim Taylor (tying shoe), and Bart Starr.

Henry Lefebvre Collection of the Neville Public Museum of Brown County

My hero! A copy of this publicity photo of Paul Hornung, or one very much like it, hung on my bedroom wall throughout my teenage years.

SUNDAY

In Green Bay during the season, the week builds toward Sunday. It's all about the game. The faithful attend church in Packer garb, and clergymen are obliged to make their sermons brief. A couple of hours before kickoff, police close the streets and turn two-way streets into one-way thoroughfares, to facilitate getting to the stadium.

When I was little, I hated Sundays because my parents went to the Packer games and left me at home with a sitter. But even then, I'd page through the programs they brought home. These were home-grown affairs rather than the standardized books the league puts out today, and they included pictures and biographies of all the players. I'd savor the sounds of the unfamiliar names: Tony Canadeo, Deral Teteak, Babe Parilli, Breezy Reid, John Martinkovic. *I used to think that last guy had* three *names*.

One day my parents had an extra ticket and asked if I would like to come along. I'd never had much interest in sports, but when they said Bob and Marcia Deutsch, who sat next to them, were bringing their daughter Robin, I decided I could make it through the afternoon.

As it turned out, I didn't spend much time chatting with Robin. I surprised myself by getting involved in the game. This was 1959, Lombardi's first season as coach. He took over a team that had been 1–10–1 the previous year and amazed everyone by winning his first three games on the way to a 7–5 record. This game was the third of the season, against the San Francisco 49ers on October 11, the day before my twelfth birthday. It was an exciting contest because the Packers led early, fell behind, but rallied to win 21–20. And halfback Paul Hornung ran for 138 yards.

I raised binoculars to see what this hero Hornung looked like, and it's not exaggerating to say my life literally changed in that second. I saw a young man who looked to me like an amalgam of Paul Newman and Elvis Presley. Wavy, blond hair; shoulders enhanced by pads under the green jersey; tight, shiny, bright-gold pants with those strategically placed laces. This was heady stuff for a preteen. Golden Boy, golden *goy*, from Notre Dame yet. I got hooked on Hornung and the Packers.

(Paul Hornung. Six feet two inches, 215 pounds. Quarterback at Notre Dame; won the Heisman Trophy despite playing on a 2–10 team. Bonus draft choice of the Packers in 1957. Lombardi switched him to halfback in 1959; he was also the team's placekicker. In 1960 he set an NFL single-season scoring record that stood for forty-six years.)

For years, the Packers played several of their home games each season in Milwaukee County Stadium. That facility held more people than City Stadium's original 32,150, and over time the Pack built a strong fan base in the southern part of the state. Dad had season tickets for both ballparks. In later years we always went down by car, stopping by Benjamin's Delicatessen for thick corned beef sandwiches to take to the game, since my parents did not care for the stadium's famed bratwurst. But the first time I was included in a Milwaukee trip, late in '59, we took the Chicago & Northwestern train. In those days pro football was so déclassé that the Packers rode the same train back from Milwaukee that we did. Since Monday was their day off, Sunday night was the time to blow off steam, and when my parents made for the club car, many of the players were there.

Dad went to get cocktails, and my mother found a place on a bench that ran down the side of the car. When she realized who was next to her, she motioned for me to squeeze in between them. There I was, sitting beside Hornung. Seeing that he was engrossed in conversation with the person on his other side, I surreptitiously ran my arm along the hem of his jacket where it touched the bench and fell away from his body, touching it with wonder and delight, delicately, too lightly to be detected.

During my teen years, home-game Sundays fell into a regular routine. The games started at one o'clock then, as I remember, before they were standardized for national television. Now all the early games start simultaneously, so it's one o'clock Eastern time, noon in Green Bay. For these one o'clock games, people would begin to gather at our home at eleven or so. We'd serve an informal brunch and head for the stadium just before noon.

Upon returning to the house, my parents would bring out some sort of hors d'oeuvres, possibly my mom's chopped liver or a creamed crabmeat recipe that Dad devised after tasting the dish in a restaurant. If I had a friend available, I'd slip out to throw the football myself for a while. Or I might retire to my room to recap the day's events in verse; every month or so I put out a little Packers newsletter. I would type my stuff laboriously on a boxy, black, secondhand typewriter—so old that its nameplate read "Corona," not "Smith-Corona"—with multiple sheets of carbon paper, and distribute the copies to a few close pals.

Then we and our guests would head out for dinner. We frequented two supper clubs: Wally's Spot downtown, and Manci's out at East Mason and Lime Kiln Road. Both were good places to encounter Packers with their wives or girlfriends. My dad was friendly with a lot of the players, so we'd stop by their tables or they'd come by ours. I remember one night my dad got into an earnest conversation with Dave Hanner, a defensive tackle from Arkansas. Dave played for the Packers for thirteen years, seven of them before Lombardi came. He's notable for playing in a game just a few days after his appendix was removed. After retirement he became a coach and then a scout; his total career with the Packers encompassed forty-four years. This was probably Dave's last year as a player, 1964, because the talk centered on his retirement. My dad, who'd had more than a few drinks, equated Hanner's fading football skills with his own ability to perform in the bedroom. That was a most unsettling conversation for his daughter to overhear.

A highlight of those evenings came when the *Press-Gazette* sportswriters, Art Daley and Lee Remmel, would enter the restaurant bearing the official statistics from the day's games. Today, with computers, it's all instantaneous. One of the Packer backs breaks a long run, and the TV sportscasters immediately tell us how many yards he's got for the day, how many for the year, where he stands in the league, and whose record he'll break if he keeps up that pace. Back then, everything had to be manually reviewed before it became official, and that took several hours. So Daley or Remmel would show up some time after eight o'clock, story filed and official stats in hand, and we'd all gather around to see if our fullback Jim Taylor had run for as many yards as Jim Brown of Cleveland.

A couple of times we ran into a player Dad knew well, and we invited him back to the house for a nightcap. Bill Forester and his wife came over on one of these occasions. Forester was a linebacker out of Southern Methodist University who played eleven years for Green Bay, served as defensive captain, was selected to four Pro Bowls, and is now in the Packers Hall of Fame. Our Siamese cat entered the room and did what cats invariably do. She found the one person in the room—Forester—who had an aversion to cats, and tried to sit in his lap. I thought it was hilarious to see the rugged football hero shrinking away from the eight-pound kitty. I stood there snickering until my mother reminded me that I was being rude and made me cart the offending feline away.

Once I started dating Gabe, I found yet another way to interact with the Packers. He would take me to Austin Straubel Field on Sunday nights to welcome the team home from their road games.

I remember in particular the aftermath of a game in 1965 against the Baltimore Colts. We didn't know it then, but it was Hornung's last big game. He had scored five touchdowns, three rushing and two receiving, and the Packers had won 42–27 on their way to the league championship. There were hundreds of people out there, but Gabe and I managed to get inside the terminal. Paul was dazzling as he entered the brightly-lit building in his green Packer sport coat, his golden hair shining and a gleaming white bandage on a broken pinky finger as he waved to the crowd. We cheered and cheered.

ONLY IN GREEN BAY

Sometimes when my friends and I go to dinner at Eve's Supper Club, we see Paul Hornung seated in the lobby, autographing books and photos. I buy whatever he is selling and chat with him a bit. Because of who and where we are, the conversation often includes one of the anecdotes in this book. He listens politely, but as I walk away, I hear him saying to whoever has accompanied him, "Can you believe that? Only in Green Bay!"

Maybe Paul, who once had his pick of the eligible females throughout the state, didn't know that he had a cadre of younger girls who adored him as well. I distinctly remember a Sunday school classmate, Marci, insisting he liked her better than me. We must have been all of thirteen at the time. Our synagogue, Cnesses Israel, collected dimes and nickels from the Sunday school kids to plant trees in Israel. When you amassed enough money for a tree, you could dedicate it to the honoree of your choice. You guessed it, there's a tree somewhere in Israel planted in honor of Paul Hornung. At least one. I wouldn't be surprised if Marci planted one too.

I used to watch for Paul's car parked on the street and wait near it for his return. Big white Cadillac, enormous fins and "Jayne Mansfield taillights," Kentucky plates; couldn't be anybody else's car.

My dad told me one day that he'd been in a tavern the previous night and had seen Paul there. He invited him back to our house and concocted a plan for Paul to come into my room, sit down on my bed, and wake me up. But a friend of Paul's came into the bar, and Paul opted to stay there and have a drink with him instead. I was extremely thankful when I heard this, since in those days I slept with huge brush rollers in my hair and calamine lotion on my acne. If I had awakened to find Paul observing me in that condition, I might have been too devastated ever to leave my bed again.

On my fourteenth birthday, my parents took me to dinner at Wally's Spot. Gary Knafelc, a movie-star-handsome receiver who later became the Lambeau Field public address announcer, was there. Gary was a friend of my dad's and greeted me, "Hiya, tiger. How's every little thing?" Upon learning that it was my birthday, without hesitation he kissed my pimply cheek. That made my day, and I will always love him for it.

I recall a story Knafelc told us: He came to the Pack from the Chicago Cardinals in 1954. His train was late, so Gary had to go directly from the station to a team meeting. In those days, everyone dressed up when they traveled, and Gary was nattily attired in a dark suit, tie, and pink shirt. As he entered the meeting, a grizzled veteran looked up at that shirt and growled, "I'll give him a week." Of course, the veteran was wrong. Gary played ten years in the league, nine of them for the Pack, and in 1976 he was inducted into the Packers Hall of Fame.

Friends ask me how my father happened to know so many Packers. I'm not sure what to tell them. I think there was a downtown businessmen's association, and my dad was active in it, so he probably met some Packers at promotional events. Some of them must have come into Newman's with their wives, to shop. And I'm sure he was introduced to some in restaurants and bars. Green Bay was pretty small in those days, only fifty or sixty thousand people, so the players weren't hard to find. Like Mount Everest, they were simply there.

Sometime in the sixties my dad came up with a forward-looking scheme to boost business. He put a ticket desk in his store. Only the Packer organization could sell their tickets, but Dad had tickets for just about all the other local events, including the ones at the Brown County Arena. Not a bad arrangement in those days before Ticketmaster and personal computers. So our family got in the habit of attending the Home and Garden Show, Holiday on Ice, the rodeo, the circus—and the Green Bay Bobcats semi-pro hockey games. A few times, we encountered Packer players taking in those games. I remember meeting rugged little defensive back John Symank there, and on another occasion linebacker Nelson Toburen, encased in plaster, recovering from the broken neck that ended his football career. The players' reactions were invariably the same: "I thought I was tough, but these guys are playing with sharp objects!"

One fine spring Sunday, my friends and I were flipping through the telephone book when we discovered that the Packers were in it, just like everyone else. Since phone books were printed only once a year and the players tended to move around, most of the addresses and numbers were out of date. But when we came upon linebacker Tom Bettis, we remembered that he was a family man who didn't leave town at the end of the season. And the book said he lived only a few blocks from Pam. We didn't dial his number. We got on our bikes and headed over to the Bettis home where we found Tom, his wife Valerie, and their two small daughters outside in the yard, engaged in a neighborhood game of softball. And we watched them until they invited us to join in.

Dad reported one day that he'd had the chance to do a favor for Jim Taylor. Taylor was the Packers' fullback in an era when the fullback was the main ball-carrier, not primarily a blocker. He rushed for over a thousand yards in five consecutive seasons, 1960–64. Slightly small for the position at six feet and 214 pounds but rock-hard, Taylor worked out incessantly when it was not yet fashionable to do so. I once heard that he'd built up his neck muscles to the point where he couldn't turn his head; he had to rotate his entire upper body to look around. Taylor had injured his back, and he came into Newman's one day wearing some sort of a wet pack in an effort to heal before the next game. The pack had sprung a leak and soaked Jim's clothing. Dad took him up to his third-floor retreat to remove the sopping thing and relax while the ladies in the store's alteration department dried and pressed his clothes.

I didn't expect to find a Packer at the Golden Arrow Archery Club. I'd enjoyed target shooting at camp, so when I became old enough to drive myself to meetings, I bought a bow and joined the club. And there was Jerry Kramer, the All-Pro guard. This was during a period when Kramer had major health issues. As a teenager in Idaho, he was chasing a calf when he ran over a sharp board. Splinters lodged in his abdomen. In 1964,

Kramer had surgery for a tumor on his liver, and missed the entire Packers season. His doctors feared he had cancer, but instead they found that some of the splinters had remained inside him for eleven years, leading to tumors and internal bleeding. During Kramer's recovery, he came to the archery club; he liked bow-hunting. He was so thin and pale that he didn't look like a football player. We all fussed over him and were delighted when he got back to normal.

So Paul is right. Green Bay, aka Titletown, USA, really is different from any other place. For most of its citizens, football is of prime importance. The story about the Packer fan at Lambeau Field, sitting next to an empty seat because all of his friends are attending his wife's funeral, is apocryphal. However, it is absolutely true that when my father suffered a cardiac episode one Sunday morning and was taken to the hospital, and I relayed that news to his friends, their first, incredulous reaction was, *"Sid missed the Bear game?"*

I read this tale in the news a few years ago, and I'm pretty sure it's legitimate. A Green Bay couple unwisely left their young child alone when they went out for a Saturday night of partying. They returned to find an official form stating that Social Services had taken their child into custody. When they hadn't tried to claim the kid by Sunday afternoon, the agency contacted them. They explained that they fully intended to pick up the youngster—but were waiting till after the game.

My friends and I lived through some of the most dramatic events of the twentieth century, but I don't think they touched us much. We felt insulated in our small, Midwestern town. I don't remember ever doing a "duck-and-cover," the infamous exercise of the fifties that would have proved totally futile in case of a nuclear attack. We booed when the Russians sent up *Sputnik*, but contentedly chewed the lumpy, blue gumballs that came on the market bearing the satellite's name. Our teachers brought radios into our classrooms when Alan Shepard ascended into space, just as they had a few years earlier when the Milwaukee Braves won the World Series. But I remember almost nothing about the Bay of Pigs, and when the wall went up in Berlin, my friends and I felt it most keenly as Packers Paul Hornung, Boyd Dowler, and Ray Nitschke were called up to newly-activated Army Reserve units.

And in those dark days of November 1963, when President John Kennedy was assassinated, amid all those questions about whether there was a conspiracy and what might happen to our nation, the one asked most frequently in Green Bay was:

Will Sunday's game be cancelled?

It was, and rightly so. But history didn't impact us directly for several more years, when our boyfriends and husbands began to leave for Vietnam and we knew our protected childhoods were over.

My friend Stacy, a high-school teacher, asked me a few years ago if I'd allow one of her students to interview me. Her social studies class was collecting oral histories of the sixties. Naturally, I wanted to talk about the assassination, and I was delighted, checking my scrapbook, to find I'd saved most of the *Press-Gazette* coverage of Kennedy's death. But one clipping puzzled me. Why would I have kept an article from one year *after* the assassination? I flipped it over and had to chuckle. On the reverse side was an ad for a Jantzen sweater modeled by Paul Hornung.

Our holidays always had a Packer flair. Through 1963, the Thanksgiving Day game was invariably Green Bay vs. Detroit. Lombardi hated the short work week, but it made great fun for us. My parents and I would watch first the Macy's parade and then the Packers and Lions on TV, amid the wonderful smells of the turkey roasting. Then we'd pack up the cooked bird and take it to the Deutsches' for dinner and a rehash of the game.

One year Bob and Marcia must have been out of town, because my father proposed something different. The Packers were scheduled to return from the game in Detroit and have dinner together, with their families, at the Elks' Club. Dad was an Elk, so he thought we could join them. Pam, who'd had her family celebration earlier in the day, came with us. But alas, as we tried to enter the club, an employee came up and announced that it was closed to everyone but the Packers. I don't know why my parents hadn't anticipated that. Neither Pam nor I can remember what we did for Thanksgiving dinner that year, but it may well have resembled the famous Chinese restaurant scene in the movie *A Christmas Story*.

There was no lengthy playoff schedule then. The season ended in mid-December. But if the Packers made the NFL championship game—and under Lombardi, they did that six times in nine years—the players would have to stay in Green Bay over Christmas, and we could use our vacation to hunt for them. We made up Packer lyrics to the old carols:

> We the Pack of Titletown are.
> Winning games, we traverse afar.
> Hornung, Taylor, Moore, and Dowler,
> Following yonder Starr.

Here's one from Carla and Del that preceded the '61 championship game against the Giants:

> God rest ye merry, Packer fans,
> Let nothing you despair.
> Remember when we play New York,
> Paul Hornung will be there
> To save us all from Tittle's power
> When we have gone nowhere.
> Oh-oh, tidings of victory and cash, victory and cash—
> Oh-oh, tidings of victory and cash!

I think that was the year I first heard the expression "Titletown, USA." The Pack had won six championships, but it had been a long time since the last one in 1944. Hopes were high before the '61 championship game, and the media started to use the term. The New York sportswriters joked that after the game, Green Bay would be re-christened "Tittletown" after the great Giant quarterback, Y.A. Tittle, but they were wrong to the tune of 37–0. By 1967, when I had a summer job working for WJPG Radio, everyone knew about Titletown. The station changed its call letters to WNFL and promoted the change with the slogan, "There's a new title in Titletown."

The Packers themselves are unique among sports franchises. If you follow football, you know this already, so I'll keep my explanation brief.

While the early professional football teams all started out in small cities such as Canton, Ohio, and Decatur, Illinois, the Packers are the only team that stayed in one. They were established in 1919 by Earl "Curly" Lambeau—player-coach until 1929 and head coach until 1949—and *Green Bay Press-Gazette* editor George Calhoun. Lambeau's employer, the Indian Packing Company, sponsored the team that first year and gave it the name "Packers." The NFL was formed in 1920, and the Packers entered the league in 1921. When the team suffered financial reverses in '22, A. B. Turnbull, general manager of the *Press-Gazette*, rallied a group of local businessmen ("The Hungry Five") behind the team and formed the Green Bay Football Corporation. So the team has been community-owned almost from the start.

Each time the Packers required a financial boost—simply to stay in business, or more recently for stadium renovation—the corporation sold stock. The Packers currently have over one hundred thousand stockholders. While a single owner can move his team for profit, there's no way all those stockholders will ever agree to pull that franchise out of Green Bay. Moreover, all the money the Packers earn goes back into the team, not into an owner's pocket. If the corporation ever is dissolved, the assets will go to a charitable foundation. In today's era of big-business sports, Green Bay is very special.

My father bought a share in the 1950 stock offering. I inherited that share and bought stock on my own in 1997. I don't receive dividends, and I can't tell the coach what to do, but I own a small piece of the club. Each year I'm invited to the annual meeting, and I vote to elect the board of directors. So I can say that the Packers are truly my team. Sometimes I even take the credit when they win.

SOME TALES OF TICKETS

Green Bay may be a small city, but the Packers draw their fan base from all over the state—actually, from all over the country and the world. Lambeau Field is always sold out with season tickets, and has been since 1960. I read recently that the waiting list for tickets has grown to eighty-one thousand names—for a stadium that seats 72,928. Tickets can be willed to family members or passed on to successor executives in a business, but there are strict limitations. So it's no wonder that ownership is sometimes contested dramatically.

Back in the seventies, a bitterly-divorced couple who belonged to our synagogue continued to meet Sunday after Sunday, year after year, at Lambeau Field. They rarely had anything to say to each other beyond, "Go Pack," but she wasn't going to give his new wife the satisfaction of taking over her seat!

Our fathers all used to have season tickets—prime locations, too. One by one, they gave them up, so today my friends and I are obliged to buy our game packages from a tour company. The saddest story involved Pam Monaghan's sister Sheila. The tickets were fifty-yard-line seats that had belonged to Pam and Sheila's parents. When their father died and their mother became too infirm to attend games, the subscription passed to Sheila and her husband, Tim. That was fine with Pam, since she lived in Louisiana and rarely made the trip north, while her sister was in Wisconsin. But then Sheila and Tim were divorced. As they divided their assets, the perfidious Tim insisted the tickets were his. He was willing to make other concessions, but only if he could have the seats.

The Packer office was of no help in straightening out the mess. "When tickets belong to a couple," they said, "we list them under the husband's name. Besides, Tim's been writing the checks."

Finally, to end the ordeal, Sheila gave in. Pam feels cheated because she never had a chance to claim her parents' seats. We still talk occasionally—only half kidding—about finding Tim, holding him up, and taking the tickets. Or going to his seat during a game and making a huge scene to embarrass him.

And then there's the tale of my childhood playmate Marilyn. A psychologist, professor, and author, Marilyn had a bicoastal career. She practiced in New York and taught in California. When her parents passed on, Marilyn inherited their Packer season tickets. After some discussion, she and her husband, an interior decorator, concluded they could follow their career paths anywhere. So Marilyn moved, with her family, back to the Green Bay area. The idea of raising teenage sons in bucolic Wisconsin, rather than New York, must have been an appealing part of the decision—but to put it in the simplest terms, they moved back to use the tickets!

THE FROZEN TUNDRA

I attended the Ice Bowl, the fabled NFL championship game played at Lambeau Field between the Packers and the Dallas Cowboys on New Year's Eve, 1967, with a kickoff temperature of thirteen below. Perhaps fortunately, I have almost no memory of this game. I guess it's like childbirth. Once the pains subside, the memories fade, or you'd never do it again. In fact, in the few flashes that cross my mind, I'm sitting in the end zone, watching the famous quarterback sneak with which Bart Starr won the game behind the blocks of Jerry Kramer and Ken Bowman. And I know we didn't have end zone tickets, so I'm recalling the film clip, not the reality.

Dad owned season tickets on the fifty-yard line and the thirty, and I think I was on the thirty, squeezed into a two-person, insulated stadium bag with my then boyfriend, now husband, Scott. The one thing I clearly remember involves a pint of my father's favorite cognac, Courvoisier, which he gave Scott and me to help keep us warm during the game. We didn't want to drink it up too early, so we waited until the end of the first quarter before bringing it out, and then—although Scott had kept it in a deep inside pocket of his coat—that first swallow went down cold all the way, like a well-iced Coke on a summer day.

I recall that six years earlier, before the '61 championship game against the Giants, the temperatures in Green Bay stayed close to zero for days, maybe as much as two weeks. But game day was practically balmy, with temps around twenty degrees. After we beat Tittle and his vaunted Giants,

I almost injured myself taking a victory leap off a three-and-a-half-foot bank of snow in the stadium parking lot.

People in warmer climates—or cities with domed stadiums—have to wonder how Cheeseheads survive those cold-weather games. Frankly, I don't think I could last out there anymore. My friends and I always pick an early-season game. After decades in Louisiana, Pam thinks even fifty degrees is frigid. I remember attending cold-weather games in Milwaukee back in the sixties, when County Stadium had a bigger capacity than Lambeau and the Packers earned extra revenue by playing a portion of the schedule there. It was a big deal for my mom and me to go to County Stadium for a late-season game because in those days, the ladies' bathrooms there were heated and the ones in Green Bay weren't. Mom copped out a couple of times and spent the second half huddling in the warmth of the restroom.

We do learn to dress for the weather—lots of layers, of course, and I like to put plastic bags inside my boots, for insulation. In the sixties, though, women were generally expected to dress up for games. The Packers always opened the season against the Bears, and that was when the ladies brought out their new fall outfits, to show them off. My parents' store did a lot of business in the week before the Bear game. But those rules went out the window when the temperature dipped—unless, of course, your fashion trophy was a mink coat. Such coats were not yet considered politically incorrect. In fact, Lombardi gave them as gifts to the players' wives and mothers after one of the championship seasons.

One pleasant development was the popularity of fashions inspired by the 1965 movie *Doctor Zhivago.* The film had Julie Christie, playing Lara, running around wintry Russia in fur-trimmed coats and big fur hats. So for a couple of years, we all got to wear replicas of her costumes, look trendy, and still keep warm. My Lara coat was bright green with frog-style fasteners, and the faux-fur trim and matching hat were white.

The coldest game I clearly remember wasn't in Wisconsin. It was the 1962 NFL championship, a rematch between the Packers and Giants at Yankee Stadium. It was thirteen above, with ferocious wind gusts—up to forty miles per hour, according to Pro Football Hall of Fame records.

The Pack stayed with a running game featuring their rugged fullback, Jim Taylor. A defensive standout, linebacker Ray Nitschke, got the Corvette that *Sport* magazine awarded to the most valuable player. The good guys won, 16–7.

I find that contest memorable for other things besides the weather. I was fifteen that year, and my father took me to New York on a charter flight the day before the game. We stayed at the team hotel, and when we got there, my dad invited the stewardesses from our plane to join us in our room for a few drinks. I was delighted, since I reasoned that their presence might attract a couple of the players. I suspect Dad invited them for another reason. He might have claimed he was recruiting models for the next Newman's fashion show, and indeed, I later saw a darkly exotic "stew" named Sandy in one of the shows.

We didn't nab Hornung as I'd hoped, but Dad's pal Lew Carpenter came down for a libation. Dad called room service for a bottle of Early Times for him. We had half of it left the next day, and Dad asked me to put it into my suitcase for the flight home. It shattered in there, leaving me to explain why I was returning a copy of Robert Graves' *I, Claudius* to the East High library reeking of bourbon.

In *When Pride Still Mattered,* his scholarly tome on Vince Lombardi, David Maraniss told a story about Lombardi's daughter that saddened me when I read it. Vince and his wife, Marie, went out for dinner on the night before that game, leaving Susan behind with a room-service tray. Although this suited her, she accidentally locked herself out of the room when she put her finished tray outside the door. Barefoot and too embarrassed to get into the elevator that way, Susan ran down twenty-six flights of stairs to the mezzanine floor, where she located her older brother, and he disgustedly got her a new key. Susan went back to her room "a wreck," fearing her father's wrath, but he merely laughed when he heard what had happened.

As I read this anecdote, it struck me that we were in the same hotel that night, and I was Susan's age. If we'd known she was alone, Dad and I might have invited her to come to dinner with us and my grandparents. Granted, Susan and I were not friends, and despite having New York backgrounds in common—they discovered they'd briefly attended a certain elementary school together—our dads were not friends. I recognized Susan when I saw her on the street, but I'm not sure she knew my name. She went to parochial schools, St. Matthew's through eighth grade and then St. Joseph's Academy, so our paths rarely crossed. My friends and I thought she was stuck-up, but she was probably just wary that anyone making overtures of friendship was doing so because of her famous father. I admit—*well, yeah*—that would have been my motive. But who knows? Susan would have had a good meal and company, and maybe we would have found some common ground. And the painful incident would have been avoided.

Sunday morning dawned with the news that Coach Lombardi and Paul Hornung were attending Mass at St. Patrick's Cathedral, which I could see from my hotel room window. I added the cathedral to my mental file of places for Packer-hunting.

One more highlight of that remarkable weekend followed the game. The Packers had their own chartered plane, but the reporters were on our return flight rather than theirs. I worked on my high-school newspaper and was considering a career in journalism, so I admired Art Daley and Lee Remmel from the *Green Bay Press-Gazette* almost as much as I admired the Packers. Remmel put a portable typewriter on his airline seat tray, and I was able to peek over his shoulder and watch him craft his story. He had a distinctive style with lots of big words and alliteration—"Bunyanesque Alabama alumnus" is a typical phrase that sticks in my mind. Remmel moved from the *P-G* to become the Packers' public relations director, assumed the title of Packer historian in his eighties, and finally retired at the end of 2007. He's still one of my heroes.

WHAT WE LEARNED FROM THE PACKERS

It's hard to describe what Lombardi meant to our town. I can't remember the name of one Green Bay mayor or Allouez town supervisor of that era, but I sure remember Vince. You could say he was the unofficial mayor. He had such a presence. You didn't have to like him, but you had to respect him.

He was coach and general manager, and once he got established, he went beyond football and gave seminars for corporate executives, teaching them how to run their businesses the way he ran his team. He was dedicated to excellence. The main lesson I remember is that he didn't focus on an opponent's weakness. Instead, he looked for their strength and attacked them there. If the Packers executed perfectly, the opposition couldn't beat them. We'd take away their best weapon and leave them nothing to use against us.

In 1959, Head Coach Vince Lombardi inherited a team that had gone 1–10–1 the year before. The Pack could claim six league championships in their history, but they hadn't even had a winning season since 1947. Vince took the Packers to a 7–5 record that first year. In 1960 the Pack went 8–4 and narrowly lost to the Philadelphia Eagles in the NFL championship game. Then came the real run: league titles in '61–'62 and '65–'66–'67, plus victories in the first two Super Bowls in 1967 and '68. Over nine years in Green Bay, Lombardi's record was 98–30–4.

In addition to coaching winning football, Lombardi sought to improve the public image of his players. There's no denying that football attracts some rough types, and in the years just prior to his arrival, the Packers had abysmal records: 3–9 in 1957 and 1–10–1 in 1958. This combination of off- and on-field performance caused many citizens to regard the players as losers and bums. But Lombardi expected his players to be gentlemen. When they went out in public to represent the club, he required them to dress in official, green sport coats. He had other rules as well. In *When Pride Still Mattered,* David Maraniss related that Lombardi automatically fined any player caught standing at a bar. Players were allowed to sit at a table and drink, but standing at a bar did not fit Lombardi's idea of a professional image. Years later, basketball star Charles Barkley argued that pro athletes should not be considered role models. Lombardi knew that his players could not escape that responsibility, and he prepared them accordingly.

My friends and I grew up with jokes about Vince taking his morning constitutional, going out for a walk on the Fox River. And the one about the heavenly football game with the figure running up and down the sideline, shouting orders to his team: "That's God. He thinks he's Lombardi."

We girls didn't exactly have a personal relationship with Vince. That stocky, commanding figure with his bulldog face and demeanor—we mostly stayed out of his way. We weren't totally stupid.

Vince was one heck of a role model, and so were most of his players. When they eventually retired, we saw them use Lombardi's principles to succeed in fields away from football. Willie Davis built a broadcasting empire. Ken Bowman became an attorney. Bob Long—of whom a teammate once told me, "He does everything slow but catch passes"—was speedy enough to get in on the ground floor with Pizza Hut and make millions on his franchises. Not exactly the "dumb jocks" some people might picture.

Lombardi's Packers weren't perfect, but they were darn near close. On the rare occasions when they lost a game, we could be sure that Vince would make them work a little harder, and they'd take the next one. Their hard work and their success were constants in our lives. They made Green Bay more than the small Midwestern town it was, and I think they made us more than what we were as well.

I identified with the Packers when I joined the East High debate team. Debating not only provided a substitute for organized sports—there were no girls' teams then—it also allowed me to ride a bus to weekend meets and earn a varsity letter, just as the male athletes did. In debate, it was imperative to appear poised and confident. I had a favorite sweater that was adorned with a large, yarn tassel. It was always a temptation to worry and twist that tassel, running my fingers through the strands, but I knew this behavior would cost me points on the podium. Instead of putting the sweater away during debate season, I consciously applied the Lombardi philosophy and gave myself an extra obstacle to overcome. I wore that sweater to all of the competitions. I knew that if I could just keep my hands off the tassel, I would use them properly.

The Packers enlarged our world in other ways. Take geography. Dave "Hawg" Hanner hailed from Arkansas. A big, ruddy-faced man with a plug of tobacco tucked in his cheek, he would have looked at home in bib overalls. He was the only person from Arkansas that we knew, so for us, he was Arkansas. Forrest Gregg, Tommy Joe Crutcher, Doug Hart, and Donny Anderson brought a taste of Texas to Green Bay. Boyd Dowler, born in Wyoming, educated at Colorado, and one of the tallest Packers at six feet five inches, was a proper son of the towering Rockies. Paul Hornung came from Louisville, so we watched the Kentucky Derby on television each May, and pictured him there.

There had to be a downside to our exposure to these charismatic people. The Packers totally spoiled me for any appreciation of sports below the professional level. I discovered this when Allouez School organized a basketball team of seventh- and eighth-grade boys. Seeing my male classmates in their uniform shorts, their legs resembling nothing more than pink noodles, only embarrassed me. Adding to my disappointment, both the East High Red Devils and the Northwestern Wildcats fielded losing football teams throughout my tenure at those schools. No one measured up to the Pack.

The same applied to my social life. In three years of dating, Gabe and I discovered a lot of common ground. We believed we were in love and talked of marriage. But my first attraction to him wasn't the fact that he was good-looking, smart, or Jewish. Rather, he was tall, and he looked a bit like a certain Packer player who'd recently broken my heart. It took me a long time to stop making those comparisons.

TIMES (*THANKS, BOB!*) A-CHANGIN'

"I can be so shy, inconsequential.
I can be a star beyond a doubt.
I've got real executive potential
If I just let it out.

I can be a floozy or Madonna.
I can be a feminist or slave.
I can be most anything I wanna.
Just tell me what you crave.
Let me know what you crave!"

Michelle to John, "I Can Be," *Third and Long*

ME AND MR. A

The sobs exploded up from my gut, loud and wrenching and thoroughly undignified. I had never cried so hard. My current Packer favorite had just ordered me out of his life. It was the worst thing I'd experienced in my almost-seventeen years. I totally lost control. Finally, drained after a half-hour of weeping, I ventured out of the music practice room at Saint Norbert College and saw a host of concerned faces. Whoops—wouldn't you think they'd make those practice rooms soundproof?

Today I see the player had justice on his side. (I'll call him Mr. Anonymous, since I view him as a private person. He was never a household name like Hornung or Starr, and unlike many retired players who go into broadcasting or front restaurants and car dealerships, Mr. A—as far as I know—has stayed out of the public eye.)

The term "stalker" wasn't part of the national vocabulary back then. And of course I meant Mr. A no harm. What pissed him off was that when I greeted him that night at the Packers' training camp at Saint Norbert College in De Pere, I had just stepped out of a bush. *Wait, I can explain!* I was hiding in the bush so Mr. A's teammates wouldn't see me and tease him about me. That's what they had done the week before when they saw us talking in the Sensenbrenner Hall parking lot. In my mind, I was doing it for him.

Three of the most wonderful weeks in my existence had just come to a crashing end. When Pam and I showed up at Packer practice that year, things had changed from previous seasons. You've seen the perennial video clips of kids loaning their bikes to the Packer players, to traverse the long slope between Lambeau Field and the practice fields across the street? We lived too far from the stadium to bring our bikes. But now, in 1964, we had driver's licenses! My parents had given me a secondhand Oldsmobile the previous Christmas, and Pam could usually borrow her mother's Chevy Corvair.

After practices, the players sweated into my cloth upholstery until my dad threatened to take my car away because of the odor. "But, Dad," I explained, "this is Packer sweat!" One day as we drove back to the locker room, Jesse Whittenton, the great defensive back, playfully leaned over and yanked my ignition key right out of the socket. Still a novice driver, I stomped on the brake in horror, convinced the car would self-destruct. I didn't know anyone could do that, and of course they can't on today's cars. My Olds rocked with the players' laughter.

Paul Hornung was on the scene, having returned from a year's suspension for gambling. (The word on the street was that everybody did it, but the league made scapegoats out of Hornung, its foremost offensive star, and defensive standout Alex Karras of the Detroit Lions. My friends and I proclaimed the first day of Paul's suspension "The Mornung of Mournung for Hornung," and I wore a black armband to school.) But although I'd scribbled in a spiral notebook just a couple of years before,

"Mind and heart can only sing,
Paul, my Paul, is everything,"

Hornung now seemed remote, inaccessible, and at twenty-eight—*dare I say it?*—old. My attention turned in a new direction.

Just out of college and only five years older than we were, this year's crop of rookies didn't treat us as children. There was a chance these guys could be had—maybe not now, but soon. We not only piled them into our cars for the trip across the stadium parking lot, we also dropped Mr. A and his buddy off at the furniture store and took them on brief tours of their new hometown. In the late afternoons and evenings, we'd take our dogs over to the St. Norbert campus for walks. The campus was in West

De Pere, just along the far side of the Fox River, and it had a beautiful area where weeping willow trees dipped down to the water. We figured the players wouldn't know we didn't live in the neighborhood, and they might miss their own dogs and come to pet ours. Sometimes we'd drive, and sometimes we'd walk the dogs the two-and-a-half miles just to get there. My big collie-shepherd mix, Pauline, enjoyed those walks, but Pam's fat, aging beagle would struggle. We usually ended up carrying Lady.

One day I had the dogs on leash, waiting for Pam to come out of the restroom, when I heard her scream. Since St. Norbert was a Catholic college, we often saw nuns and priests on the campus. Nuns mostly wore the long, traditional habits in those days, and some of these wore all-white robes instead of black-and-white ones. A white-clad nun had come around a corner in the ladies' room, and Pam thought for a moment she was seeing a ghost. I teased her unmercifully for the rest of the afternoon. It wouldn't have been so funny if she hadn't been Catholic.

Pam was always the social one. I'd let her make the connections, while I'd hang back. One day we were in her car when we saw Mr. A and a friend on the campus. She waved and yelled hello. We'd talked to them at practice earlier that day, so I was embarrassed to turn up again so soon. As Pam called out, I dived to the floor of the car, only to look up and hear Mr. A saying, "What are you doing down there?" I pretended I'd lost a contact—a flat-out lie, since I didn't get my first, cherished lenses till the next Christmas.

I'll never forget the first time I saw Mr. A. I was hanging around the players' exit, waiting for autographs and hellos. Unfortunately I was too easily satisfied with hellos, or I'd be making a fortune on eBay today. A third of that team is in the Hall of Fame.

And this huge rookie stepped out. He was lean by today's standards for linemen, but one of the biggest people around that day. And he smiled. No kidding, he had the most amazing smile. I felt an instant physical reaction. I was surprised to find myself still on my feet. I could swear I'd felt myself go over onto my bottom. "Wow," said an old man next to me. "That one looks like the Jolly Green Giant!"

I'd never felt anything like that before. I wanted to climb that big man like a jungle gym.

Pam and I used to conduct our own little draft after the rookie list came out in the spring. We'd pick out players we wanted to get to know. I was pleased that the Green Giant was one of mine.

The first thing I ever baked in my life was a batch of chocolate chip cookies for Mr. A. I wasn't into cooking then; Frances took care of that. I had a recipe that called for walnuts, and I got to the store and didn't know the difference between black walnuts and English walnuts. I bought the black ones and made the cookies with them. I thought they tasted kind of unusual, but I brought them to the stadium anyway. Mr. A didn't say anything besides "Thank you," but Henry Jordan, the All-Pro defensive tackle, noticed, and told me they were special and delicious. Henry was always sweet to us kids. I don't think I've tasted black walnuts since, and I don't know whether their flavor that day was good or whether these were a bit "off."

Back to that fateful night. It was almost time for curfew, and there I was in the parking lot. It was the night of the second-to-last roster cuts. If Mr. A's car didn't pull into that lot, it would mean he'd been dropped from the team. Finally, there it came! And I stepped out of that bush to congratulate him. But now Mr. A wasn't smiling.

Part of the problem was that we didn't speak the same language. When I said, "I want you to meet my parents," I was thinking, "My dad's friends with lots of Packer players. If you become his friend, I'll get to see more of you." He heard it as, "She's getting serious and she's underage!" I didn't have any delusion that at seventeen, I could become Mr. A's girlfriend. I could see myself as part of his life, but as a little sister or mascot figure. *Until the day straight out of the movies, when he'd look at me and see that I was all grown up ...*

Maybe we should have recognized our differences a week or two earlier. My parents took Pam and me to the Midwest Shrine exhibition game at County Stadium in Milwaukee. We arrived very early, and exploring the stadium, we came upon the area where the players pass from their locker rooms onto the field. I was fresh from a summer drama course at Northwestern University's National High School Institute, and now I was serving on the makeup committee for St. Norbert's summer musical.

Steeped in theater, I found it natural, as Mr. A came through the passage, to chirp the time-honored good-luck wish, "Break a leg!" Mr. A gave me a very strange look. He had evidently spent his school career doing jock things instead of fine arts. He didn't know the term.

Fortunately, he didn't break a leg.

He pulled a hamstring.

* * *

You may think this was the end for us, and it probably should have been. But Mr. A was destined to move in and out of my life.

In 1966, I was a sophomore at Northwestern University. My boyfriend Gabe, who by now had moved back to Green Bay, came to visit me on the weekend of the Packer-Bear game in Chicago. We were in downtown Chicago on Saturday night and thought it would be fun to stop in at the Drake Hotel, where the Packers were staying. I wore a black knit sheath dress with ruffles around its long sleeves and V-neck. The short skirt showed off my trendy, black stockings with their woven diamond pattern. High heels and a pearl choker completed my ensemble. I wanted to look nice for Gabe, but that wasn't my main purpose in dressing up. I knew that if Mr. A saw me tonight, he would finally find me grown up and desirable. We walked into the Drake's lobby, and the first player we saw was guard Fuzzy Thurston. Fuzzy recognized me, despite my new maturity. Oh yes, he recognized me, and his first words were, "Hey, did you hear? Old Mr. A got married this week!"

* * *

Late in my college years, my dad informed me that he had, after all, become close to Mr. A. My hero's marriage was not going well, and he would come to my father's cozy third-floor retreat to tell Dad his troubles. I wondered whether Mr. A had any idea whose father he'd befriended!

On Saturdays when I was home from NU, I'd go down to Dad's office hoping to encounter Mr. A, but I never saw him. This story smacked so much of "tell her what she wants to hear" that I wondered about my father's veracity. His little girl was off at college, slipping away from him. Perhaps he'd made it all up to get closer to me. But a few years later, when Watergate came into the news, my registered-Republican father said that what disappointed him most about President Nixon was that he'd answered falsely when his daughter Julie asked if there'd been a cover-up. "A father shouldn't lie to his daughter," mine proclaimed.

So I can only conclude that either my dad was as big a BS artist as Tricky Dick Nixon, or his friendship with Mr. A was real.

* * *

One morning after Scott and I had been married for a few years, I picked up my local paper. A familiar face smiled out from the entertainment section. Near the end of his career, Mr. A had collaborated with two sportswriters on a book, and he was plugging it. He was divorced and—oh my—living not far from us. I rushed out to buy the book, and raced through it. *Am I in it? No! Should I be disappointed? Well, at least he didn't say anything bad about me.* No matter, I was married now, and I had my own life to lead. I admit I looked up his address in the phone book, and I drove past his condo a few times, but I never saw him.

So it doesn't count.

I AM WOMAN, WHATEVER THAT MEANS

My friends and I came together in that glossy time right before all the rules were thrown out. The early sixties were nothing like the end of the decade. Skirts were getting shorter (although we still wore them for school and trips downtown), hairstyles higher and shinier, eye makeup heavier. A raw sound was creeping into the music; sexual messages in movies and advertising became more overt. Filmgoers sighed over secret agents who drove fast cars, foremost among them James Bond. Playboy bunnies, stewardesses, and Miss America were regarded as desirable objects, although we hadn't figured out how to emulate them.

When I was a little girl playing at being a grown-up, I presumed I could be a teacher, a nurse, or a secretary. I could work in a store like my mother did, but since everyone else had stay-at-home moms, I didn't want to be like her. If I grew up to be pretty, I could be a stewardess, who was a sex object offering "Coffee, tea, or me?" Or since I had some writing ability, maybe I could become a spunky girl reporter like Brenda Starr or Lois Lane. And aside from "housewife," those were all the choices that I perceived I had.

And then women's lib arrived, and they told us we could be anything we wanted. We could be engineers, race-car drivers, astronauts. *(Carla might have made one hell of an astronaut.)* We liked the idea that we were as good as men and could do anything they did, but we weren't always sure about how to proceed.

Also in the sixties came the sexual revolution, and what did we know? Our mothers didn't talk to us about sex, and if they did, the talk was brief and not always accurate. I'd be dead if I'd followed my mother's instructions for inserting a tampon. Most of what we knew, we picked up from our peers—and a bit from the copy of *Catcher in the Rye* that Del's mother bought her, thinking it was a baseball story.

I remember Del's calling me after a date when we were well into our teens, hot to know why the boy had asked when she'd last had her period. Years later, Pam was put in the interesting position of having to explain—not to her mother, but to her mother-in-law—exactly what it was that Monica Lewinsky did for President Clinton. Nathalie's reaction: "Who'd want to do that?"

Athletics was one area where girls were definitely regarded as the weaker sex. My friends and I loved sports, but in those days before Title IX, there really weren't any athletic programs for girls. My high school offered GAA, Girls' Athletic Association, which was a hyped-up name for after-school intramurals. Basically we played the same games we did in gym class, wearing the same hideous, flamingo-red gym suits with bloomer legs. And we played by girls' rules. In basketball, for instance, we had six players on a side, not five, and we played half-court. Only two designated "rovers" on each team were allowed to cross the center line.

Whenever we did any sort of exercise, we were warned to be careful so we wouldn't wind up with big muscles like the boys. It was admirable to be a dedicated dancer or ice skater, but definitely uncool to have it result in overdeveloped thighs.

I had always been among the last kids picked for teams. But now that I'd discovered sports, I was anxious to play as well as watch them. In eighth or ninth grade, my school introduced the Presidential Fitness Tests. I had assumed this was something President Kennedy thought up—he was always playing touch football, right?—but I Googled it recently and found out it had started under Eisenhower. It was part of our national craze to keep up with the Russians after they launched *Sputnik*. I was horrified when the testing began, to find that despite all my hours watching the Packers and playing touch football and softball with my new friends, I couldn't perform a single one of the sit-ups mandated by the program. I started doing calisthenics every night, and by my senior year in high school, I could do a hundred sit-ups. I never did learn to climb a rope, though.

All of those summers I spent at camp, I struggled with the Red Cross swimming certifications. I'd mastered the strokes, but diving terrified me. Finally I managed to upend myself, fall head-first into the water, and qualify for my Swimmer's card. Now I had the prerequisite for a lifesaving course, so when Carla wanted to take one at the Green Bay YMCA, I joined her. I aced the written tests, but never had enough upper-body strength to be any good at the rest. Carla called me one afternoon to say she'd just bought a two-piece suit and wanted to wear it to class. But she didn't want to be the only one in a two-piece, so would I wear mine?

Now, these weren't bikinis. They were modest affairs, more like a halter top and shorts, in demure, plaid fabrics. Even so, I didn't think a two-piece was practical for lifesaving class. But Carla was so insistent that I agreed.

Our instructor was a small but muscular young man named Clyde. In my mind, he didn't measure up to the Packers, but he was fine to look at in his tight, red trunks. My assignment that night was to "save" him in a mock drowning. It was a long struggle, but I finally got him back to the shallow end, where we stood up. To my horror, I found that the top of my two-piece suit had worked itself up, and my left breast was pointing straight at Clyde. To this day, I'm certain that Clyde awarded me my lifesaving certificate only to ensure we wouldn't repeat that experience.

My senior year, East High and West High decided to form girls' track teams. We were the only schools that had teams, so we had one meet, held at East in the former Packer stadium. There was a nice cinder track that went around the football field. I was never fast, but I'd worked myself into shape, so I hoped to make up for my lack of speed with stamina. I volunteered for the half-mile run. Alas, I could not compete in this event, since no one from West High was training for a distance so great. Instead I joined Carla, Del, and another girl on a relay team, and we won.

I always got a thrill walking into East High's stadium. It had been the Packers' stadium from 1925–56, so it had only been a few years since they moved out. I didn't watch the games before 1959, but I knew the names of stars, including halfback Tony Canadeo and quarterback Tobin Rote, who'd performed during the fifties on that field. Now, there I was, literally walking in their footsteps.

Canadeo was part of my life long before I appreciated the Packers. When I was a toddler, someone gave me a tiny doll dressed in a football uniform. He didn't wear Packer colors, but he sported the great runner's number three, so my parents taught me to call him Tony Canadeo, and I kept him propped up on the small lamp I used as a night-light.

My dad took me and Judy to the dedication of new City Stadium in 1957. It was a big deal for Green Bay, with Miss America, TV star James Arness, and Vice President Richard Nixon in attendance. The festivities started at the old facility. Huge, flower-bedecked floats circled the field and then proceeded across the river to the new stadium on the West Side. The new ballpark was called City Stadium until 1965, when Curly Lambeau died and it was renamed in his honor. It originally was a couple of tall, gray, concrete slabs joined by low semicircles at the ends, and it seated 32,150. It has been enlarged and renovated several times, and now 72,928 of the faithful can pack in behind its handsome brick shell. In the early days there was a children's section where Carla and Del, among others, could get general-admission seats for, I think, as little as a dollar. Today the games are always sold out, and the cheapest end-zone tickets in 2011 list for sixty-nine dollars.

The old stadium next to East High—still in use by the school—has been refurbished and dedicated as a historical site.

Athletics aside, the whole perception of women was different in those days. I can barely watch the old James Bond films that I once loved to see with Gabe. There's a scene in one of them—*Goldfinger*, I believe—where Bond is at a party with a cute, blonde date. Agent Felix Leiter enters and wants to speak to him. Bond tells his girlfriend to leave them; it's time for man talk. When she objects, Bond spins her around and slaps her smartly on the bottom to send her away. *Yuk!* And this is not some chauvinist dork, this is Agent Double-Oh-Seven, Bond, James Bond, the urbane, irresistible hero of the time!

In the fall of 1967, starting my junior year in college, I decided I needed the new birth control pill. I had no resource but our family doctor, who happened to be my parents' friend and a member of our synagogue. I made an appointment to have a wart removed from my finger. The wart was real, but as the doctor assembled his instruments, I hit him with my request for the pill. He was clearly shocked and asked if I were already sexually active. When I said yes, he grudgingly wrote the prescription, but only after a long lecture about how the boy was using me and would soon disappear now that he'd gotten what he wanted. I was turning twenty, well past the age of consent, so ethically he couldn't alert my parents. Fortunately, he was wrong about "the boy," who eventually married me.

At least, all we had to worry about in those days was pregnancy, not AIDS. As it was, I saw a couple of my friends through illegal abortions. I once drove a college friend from Evanston, Illinois, to Madison, Wisconsin, because that was the only place we could find a doctor who'd perform one.

After I graduated from college with a BS in radio, TV, and film, I worked in a series of small radio stations. To make myself more employable, I needed a first-class engineer's license. Getting one from the Federal Communications Commission meant passing an exam that concentrated heavily on electronics. I spent five weeks during the summer of 1968 at the Elkins Radio License School in Chicago, taking a cram course so I could pass that test. Everyone made a big deal about my being the only woman, but the reality was that I was taking this memorization class with a bunch of men who were just as clueless about electronics as I was.

By 1970, I was working at WEEF Radio in Highland Park, Illinois, where I did a little bit of everything. I typed up the program logs, wrote commercials, and served as key operator for the copy machine—all traditional women's work. But I was also running the control board, reading transmitter gauges, announcing the news, and occasionally filling in as a disc jockey. Our news director was Julie, a woman my age—even though research studies of the time said listeners didn't regard a female newscaster as authoritative. Julie and I got permission to present a special talk show in which we'd interview guests from NOW, the National Organization for Women. We invited Norma, a co-worker some twenty years our senior, to participate. Norma responded that she wanted nothing to do with such a program. Julie and I went ahead with the show, and I wrote and recorded a promo for it. Its tag line—which makes me squirm today—was "It may make you want to burn your bra."

My three friends and I did our best to function in our new roles. Mostly, we took baby steps. We left something for the next generation to build on, though, and it looks like we did it pretty well. I don't have a daughter, but each of my friends has at least one. Carla's older daughter runs a successful online business, and the younger one is a paralegal. One of Pam's girls is an attorney; the other is a whiz with computers. And Del's daughter—well, she works for a national women's foundation. We hear, every so often, that she's hanging out with someone like Gloria Steinem.

But if Pam and I sometimes seem confused about life, no wonder! We are products of our time, after all. We grew up on the cusp of a new era—and someone kept changing the rules.

WE'RE GETTING TOO OLD FOR THIS!

The summer of 1968 brought Pam and me some long, lonely nights. We were entering our senior year of college, and our boyfriends, who'd already graduated, were away in the army. Throughout August, Pammy and I cruised the back roads of Wisconsin on twenty-nine-cent gas, warbling "I'm So Horny" to the tune of "I Feel Pretty" from *West Side Story*. ("*Oh, it's corny how horny I feel . . .*") I got to see places like Two Rivers and Shirley that previously had only been names on a map to me.

Leaving Green Bay for college and becoming more or less engaged hadn't changed our attitude toward the Packers in the least. We were finally old enough to date them, but for some reason, almost all the single Packers at that time were African Americans. This was the time of President Lyndon Baines Johnson and civil rights milestones, but some things still weren't *de rigueur* in small Wisconsin towns. Pam and I wasted a lot of time debating whether our parents would freak out more if we went out with dark-skinned bachelors or married white guys, before admitting that neither scenario was going to fly. So we hung out with the black singles anyway, when they let us.

Pam had a summer job at the Model Cleaners and Laundry on Riverside Drive. Model charged the Packers half price, so the players flocked in and handed Pam their dirty laundry. I liked to say this gave a whole new dimension to the term "jock sniffing." Pam's eyes—enhanced by tinted contacts—were a startling shade of blue, and she knew how to flirt with them. She made lots of new friends. One was a player I'll rename Calvin.

Cal knew better than we did that there was no future in their relationship, but he let us hang around anyway, and we got to know quite a few of the African American players. It was fun to watch Travis Williams, "the Road Runner," take a kickoff back for a touchdown and tell our friends that we'd been with him just that past Wednesday—mostly trying not to eavesdrop while he made interminable, longing phone calls to his wife in California. *No danger of impropriety there!* Once we actually ventured down to Sammy's with Cal and a buddy of his who was on the Packers' taxi squad, the closest we ever came to a Packer date. The guys pooh-poohed the idea of kosher salami on a pizza, but ended up eating most of it while we picked at whatever they'd ordered.

Pam was finishing up at Mount Mary College in Milwaukee, and I was an hour and a half down the road in Evanston. My parents still had season tickets for the games at Milwaukee County Stadium, and they were willing to take us. I'd drive up and spend Saturday night with Pam, and we'd head downtown to the Pfister Hotel, the Pack's home away from home.

One incident I'd mercifully blocked out of my memory, till Pam reminded me recently, occurred at the Pfister. We'd brought along a Green Bay girl who, like Pam, had gone on to Mount Mary. I'll call her Sally. We were on one of the upper floors when we saw running back Donny Anderson going into his room. (Anderson was the heir apparent to Paul Hornung in more ways than one. Known as "the Golden Palomino," he was a handsome, blond halfback out of Texas Tech, and when he signed a three-year contract for $600,000 in 1966, it was the highest in the NFL to date. In contrast, starting salaries in the fifties tended to be in four figures, and many of the players had off-season jobs.)

Sally did something that none of us had ever dared to do before. She went right up to Anderson's door and knocked. When he opened it, we saw that he had removed his trousers and was standing there in boxer shorts. I don't remember how Anderson got rid of her, but I do know that Pam and I were mortified. We had rules about what you could and couldn't do.

And that wasn't the first time Sally had embarrassed us. Back in Green Bay, she came with us to watch practice one day. We were waiting for the players to change into street clothes, so we walked around the team's parking area and pointed out their cars to Sally. "Wow!" she exclaimed. "Tommy Crutcher drives a Grand Prix!" Only she didn't pronounce it "pree." She pronounced it like it's spelled. Yeah, she said ... *ewww* ... and she said it loudly. We concluded we couldn't take Sally anywhere.

So it was just Pam and me at the Pfister on a certain autumn evening in 1968. We knew that this was perfectly safe and we weren't sending the wrong message. Lombardi had handed over the coaching reins to Phil Bengtson, but he continued as the Packers' general manager. His presence was still strongly felt, and we knew how strict he was. And remember, our mothers had never explained the fine points of sex. On the basis of our limited knowledge, we were positive that Vince Lombardi would never, ever, let his players expend their body fluids and weaken themselves by having relations on the night before a game.

We got on the Pfister house phone and tried to locate Cal. He wasn't around, and we ended up in a room with two Packers we barely knew. But of course, this was perfectly safe because Lombardi would never let his players have sex on the night before a game!

When we entered the room, one of the players, a huge, handsome, brown-skinned fellow, was lying in his bed. His chest was bare, and his lower body was hidden by the bedcovers. Pam sat down on the bed and began to chat with him.

I somehow ended up in the bathroom, giggling and explaining to the second player that I couldn't take a shower with him because I didn't want to get my pretty outfit wet, when Pam suddenly tugged at my elbow. "We have to go!" she whispered. "We have to go *right now!*" She was quivering, her blue eyes wide. I had never seen her in such a state. I bade a reluctant farewell to my new buddy and followed Pam out the door. In the elevator, she told me what had happened. She had been giving a back rub to the big guy, feeling perfectly safe in the assurance that Lombardi—*yeah, you know*—when he, making a far more logical assumption, rolled over ...

And that is why the first male organ ever viewed by Pamela Marie Monaghan ...

Lily-white banker's daughter ...
Catholic schoolgirl ...
 Future teacher of America's youth ...
 Engaged to one of our fighting men in Vietnam ...
  Saving herself for marriage ...
  Belonged to an extremely large ...
   African American ...
    PACKER!

Cal's take on the episode, when we caught up with him the next week: "You've got to watch what you're doing. Not everybody's like me."

And that was our last visit to the Pfister Hotel.

MR. TAXI

It never really hit home that Pam and I could have gotten our heroes in trouble. Not to mention ourselves. Pammy's dad was vice president of a bank, and her mom was blatantly proud of the family's social position. Any conduct that wasn't strictly on the up-and-up involving Pam and a Packer player would have created major upheaval.

Although I'd borrowed cautionary tales about "baseball Annies" and their ilk from the Kellogg Public Library, such consequences never occurred to me or to Pam. We found the Packers fascinating, and our mission was to get as close to them as possible—in a sort of PG-rated way. (Carla and Del, wisely, had given up "hunting" by our college years.)

When she was about twenty, Pam had a flirtation going with one of the Packers' assistant coaches, a former NFL player in his late thirties. But when he invited her to join him on a weekend scouting trip, she retorted, "Is your wife going to come with us too?" We were both so naïve, we thought Coach was the bad guy. Years went by before we realized that Pam had clearly been giving him the wrong impression. And then we were horrified.

That said, I once had a chance to get a notch for my bedpost, if I'd wanted one. My prospective partner was on the Pack's taxi squad—what we'd call the practice squad today. He practiced with the team but never made the active roster. (The term "taxi squad," by the way, is attributed to Arthur B. "Mickey" McBride, who founded the Cleveland Browns in 1946. McBride kept inactive players under contract by assigning them to drive his fleet of cabs.)

Mr. Taxi, a personable African American, was a buddy of Calvin's when Pam was seeing Cal. So from time to time, the four of us would get together, but only in the most casual way.

One day—this must have been late summer '67 or '68—I asked my parents whether we could invite Cal and Mr. Taxi to have dinner at our home. My dad agreed, but I was surprised to run into opposition from other quarters. My mother was hesitant; our housekeeper, Frances, flatly refused to cook for such guests. And Pam's parents—either because they didn't realize she'd been spending the occasional evening at Cal's house *or maybe because they did*—would not allow her to attend.

I reminded Mom that my father had always made a point of inviting "Negro" Packers to our home, both because he found some of them congenial and because he knew that few others invited them. I remembered players Veryl Switzer and Nate Borden as guests at our dinner table. Evidently it was instructive for me to socialize with people of a different color when I was nine or twelve, but not when I was twenty. Not even in LBJ's Great Society. Not even when I argued that they were friends, not boyfriends.

You have to realize, Green Bay was close to 100 percent white in those days. Okay, we had a sprinkling of Native Americans, but if we saw a black person, we figured it was either a Packer or his family member or visiting friend. There was one black family in Allouez for a while—the son was in Del and Carla's grade and the daughter was younger—but I think they moved away before we left elementary school.

We finally had the dinner—without Pam, although I called to give her a report as soon as Calvin and Taxi were out the door. My dad grilled steaks in the fireplace, and we had beans from a can to accompany them. And plenty of liquor, as was customary in our home. Fran stayed in her room, and it wasn't terribly awkward. Dad, a skilled raconteur, was always great company.

A few nights later, I was home alone and heard a knock at the door. Mr. Taxi, now cognizant of my address, had stopped by for a chat. Or whatever. I had no intention of permitting much "whatever"—Scott and I were an item by this time—but I invited Taxi in. However, the evening was a failure from his point of view. Every time he tried to get anywhere near me, my big collie-shepherd mix Pauline would squeeze between us.

Jeez, even the *DOG?*

In our tiny house, there was no good place to confine the obstreperous Pauline, and if I'd chained her in the yard, she would have barked incessantly. We couldn't very well go out where people would see us together, and going to his place would definitely give him the wrong idea. "I'm so sorry," I stammered over and over. "She's never done anything like this before." But after half an hour Taxi left, disappointed.

I do have some vague memories of tumbling on a bed with Mr. Taxi in the small West-Side motel where he was staying. But I'm sure I kept my clothes on, or most of them. Taxi had a beautiful body and always smelled pleasantly, if a bit strongly, of a popular cologne. I was fascinated with the wooly texture of his hair and the delicate shading on his palms, but I was always afraid to look at him too long, thinking it was rude. What I noticed as much as his physical attributes was his watch, always set fifteen minutes ahead to "Lombardi time." Here was proof of a legend: We'd long heard that any Packer who dared to show up for a ten o'clock bus trip at ten o'clock would find that the bus had left without him!

Taxi was a sweet man, but I never considered him my intellectual equal. We had little to talk about besides football. To tell the truth, I could have gone for Cal, who seemed much smarter and had a nice, edgy wit. But I wouldn't poach on Pam's territory, no matter how tenuous her claim.

By this time I wasn't a virgin. This was the sixties, after all, and I wasn't a strict Catholic like Pam. But there was no reason to sleep with Taxi, except (a) to be able to say I'd "done it" with a Packer (*almost-Packer*), or (b) to be able to say I'd "done it" with a black man. Those reasons weren't good enough.

I've wondered from time to time whether I might have chosen differently if Taxi had been a starter instead of a practice-squad hopeful. Or if he'd been All-Pro. But I don't think so. I was probably more mature at twenty than I was a couple of decades later.

The obstreperous Pauline.

"A DRINKING TOWN WITH A FOOTBALL PROBLEM"

I can't claim authorship of this chapter title. If you go to Green Bay, you'll see plenty of T-shirts and buttons with that slogan on them, on sale racks and on people's chests. "Green Bay: A Drinking Town with a Football Problem." Of course those souvenirs are tailored to, and sold in, other markets besides Green Bay, but the slogan seems particularly fitting for my hometown. Although the game crowds were much more sedate than they are today, alcohol was clearly a part of our lives.

Quite simply, Wisconsinites enjoy their adult beverages. Our civics teacher at Allouez School used to tell us about a small, nearby town that had an official population of eight—and not one, but two thriving taverns.

Years later I learned that Wisconsin is the nation's runaway leader in brandy and cognac consumption. I joked that a lot of that was due to my father. He certainly loved his Courvoisier after dinner, and he loved his Scotch-and-soda before dinner, too, as did my mom. By the time I was seven I could mix one the way they liked it. *Put the ice in the glass, pour the Scotch up to the top of the knitted sleeve that served as a coaster, and fill the glass to the top with soda.* It wasn't a little glass, either; it was a big water tumbler, and they'd down two of them every night. Scott—who prefers his Scotch on the rocks—almost fell over when he saw the size of the first drink I poured him at our house.

Although we lived in a drinking culture, my friends and I didn't partake much while we were in high school. Shortly after I fell in with Carla and Del, we had a little party in their classmate Kris's basement. Her folks had a wine cellar, and we helped ourselves to a bottle of sherry. But we were only thirteen or fourteen, and I don't think anyone liked it much. It was just a thing to do.

I eventually got a reputation as a drinker because my folks would let me have a glass of wine with them, and because I'd bragged about tossing down a few whiskey-and-sweet-sodas at the Newman's store Christmas party the year I was sixteen. But I didn't do that sort of thing regularly. No one in my crowd did.

None of us smoked in those days, either. When we got to East High, we couldn't smoke on the campus, of course. There was a little store kitty-corner from the school across Baird Street, and the kids who indulged would go over there on their breaks. I never went in there, but I understood that the atmosphere was pretty close to solid smoke. When someone opened the door, huge clouds would waft out.

Things changed as we got near the end of high school. In Wisconsin at that time, as a nod to the beer industry, we could drink beer at eighteen. It was a rite of passage to go down and get a "beer card" at the Brown County Courthouse at Walnut and Jefferson Streets. I still have mine. It has my senior picture on it, and my legal name, Shoenthal.

I never quite forgave my dad for changing his name but not doing it legally. I guess he didn't go all the way because he was afraid of upsetting my grandfather. When I was in my teens and needed to obtain my own legal documents, I kept running up against the fact that my birth certificate said Shoenthal and I was registered in school as Shaw. To get my driver's permit, I had to take the written test twice. When I applied for a license under Shoenthal, the DMV wouldn't recognize the test I'd taken in drivers' ed as Shaw. I was all for women's lib, but there was no chance of keeping my maiden name once I was married. I was thrilled to have only one last name, even though it was my husband's.

We couldn't use the card everywhere beer was sold. There were special teen bars that catered to the eighteen-through-twenty set. They sold beer and pop; no hard liquor. Our local bar was The Prom, out in West De Pere on Highway 41. I only went there a couple of times because I had a late birthday. I didn't turn eighteen until October 1965, after I'd matriculated at Northwestern. East High had its senior class party at The Prom, and they let us seventeen-year-olds in for that one night, but without the card we couldn't buy beer.

As for marijuana, I don't think any of my high school friends would have had the slightest idea where to get it—though I'm sure Del encountered some serious tokers later, when she transferred from Denver to the University of Wisconsin after her father's death. Madison in those days was a hotbed, but Northwestern came late to all that sixties protest/drugs/free sex business. Two years after I left NU, a black woman was student body president and they were holding sit-ins, but when I went there, it was still overwhelmingly preppy.

It wasn't that my friends and I thought drinking and smoking were bad. Many of our parents did both. The first time I saw Paul Hornung up close, he had a glass of whiskey in his hand, and I was impressed when he filmed a Marlboro commercial, back when they could advertise cigarettes on TV. But smoking, especially, wasn't something we were ready to do. The kids who went to the little store were considered sort of "hoody," and they mostly weren't Allouez kids.

Allouez, at least at that time, was a place of privilege. Our suburban town, lying between Green Bay and De Pere on the east side of the Fox River, had its own school system, kindergarten through eighth, and we were told it was better than either the Green Bay schools or the parochial school system. That probably was true, because I remember ninth grade at Washington Junior High being largely a repeat of eighth at Allouez.

When we finished at Allouez, we could choose whether to go on to East Green Bay or East De Pere High. Most of us went to East Green Bay, with the ninth-grade year at Washington Junior. Carla, Del, and I all did, but Pam opted for De Pere. I suppose her parents thought she would achieve more in the smaller school. Pam confesses that she chose De Pere because she hoped to date a boy who'd selected it the year before.

A lot of Allouez students had been at school together for the whole nine years, or most of them, and we remained a unit when we got to East. Judy will tell me something about "Mary" or "Kathleen," and although there were plenty of girls with those names, I always know who she means. At an East High reunion, Del got upset because one of her friends wanted to socialize only with the Allouez kids and tried to pull her back when she greeted a pal from north of the Webster Avenue viaduct.

It seemed to me that we were even superior physically, compared to the kids from the city. At least, we matured faster. I returned to Allouez School to start seventh grade, just an inch short of my adult height, and found to my chagrin that Judy and several others had shot past me. In contrast, in high school I served as a counselor for a spring campout of Green Bay sixth-graders—something I'd never have had the courage to do without Del and Carla alongside—and most of my campers barely came up to my chest.

The first time I heard Garrison Keillor say in *A Prairie Home Companion*, "Welcome to Lake Wobegon, where … all the children are above average," I thought of Allouez.

No, we didn't all have advantages. There were some seedy neighborhoods in Allouez, but it's true enough as a generalization. The long-limbed, clean-living, favored few that we were, naturally we left school expecting to do great things. In case you're wondering, Lombardi lived in Allouez, although he sent his kids to the Catholic schools.

It probably won't surprise you that most of our parents voted Republican. Of course, we imitated them, and you could hear kids on the playground of Allouez School talking about the "Damn-o-craps." Even handsome, young President Kennedy wasn't popular with us before his assassination, although he taught us the meaning of "charisma." *I mean that literally—a lot of people my age encountered the word for the first time in the media coverage of JFK.*

It was comfortable being Republican kids in the fifties. President Eisenhower was like a kindly grandfather with the added cachet of being a war hero. Vice President Nixon had daughters our age. Today, my friends and I are all over the spectrum, and we have to pledge not to discuss politics on our yearly trips. Del actively works for the Democrats. I'm more or less apolitical, feeling that one guy is no better than the next. I've noticed that Carla "likes" Republican causes on Facebook, and after all, she's the one who's stayed closest to our roots. Pam, I'm quite sure, is conservative in all things—from her politics to her favorite Packer T-shirt, which proclaims, "Nitschke never wore an earring."

When we visit the area, my friends and I drive by East High and De Pere High, and past our old houses. We'd love to drive by Allouez School, where we spent so many years and founded our friendship. But we can't. When the baby boom ended, the old school building was torn down and a drugstore built in its place. And Allouez has been absorbed into the Green Bay school system.

By the time we got to college, drinking was an accepted part of the social scene. We dived in with enthusiasm, and sometimes we carried it off and sometimes we didn't. My friends recall an occasion when Pam visited Carla out at Carroll College in Waukesha. She tried some new beverage, enjoyed it too much, and spent most of the weekend in the bathroom. I experienced a similar evening involving the rabbi's son and a tub of Singapore Slings. Scott, playing the true friend, whisked me out of that party and back to my dorm before I could either miss curfew or throw up on my date.

In the summer of '67, I broke up with Gabe and started getting serious with Scott. He came up to Green Bay for a weekend and brought his friend Frank, who was Pam's partner for the duration. Pam suggested that we get our Saturday dinner at Rock Falls Bar, out past the city limits on the bay road that heads up to Door County. The food, she proclaimed, was inexpensive and good. The place was known for being easy—that is, no one was likely to check our IDs. "And," she told us, "they have the best drinks!"

So the four of us were heading up the bay, when I suddenly exclaimed, "Oh, no!"

"What's wrong?" Scott asked.

"I just remembered that Pam prefers cocktails where you can't taste the liquor!" Not good news at all to a Scotch-on-the-rocks drinker.

The evening was salvaged, though, because we ran into a legendary Packer at that restaurant. Pam and I were thrilled that he recognized us, and Scott still loves to tell the story of what happened next. "I want you to meet someone," I said to him. Scott turned and found himself staring at a massive chest. He tilted his head back, up, up again, as I finished the introduction, "This is Ray Nitschke."

Presumably they didn't water down Nitschke's drinks, or maybe he was on the wagon at that time. When he first came to the Packers, Ray had a reputation as a hard drinker and a brawler. But after he met his wife, Jackie, he settled down and became a solid citizen and a family man.

My mom claimed that Ray made a drunken pass at her, one night in those early days. It might have been that same night on the train when I first saw Hornung up close. "I'm old enough to be your mother!" she snapped. "Oh, you still look pretty good," Ray allegedly responded. But this is not the grown-up Ray who eventually became one of the most beloved Packers of his era.

One more reflection on drinking: Of course, I don't condone driving under the influence, and it is certainly tragic when innocent people are injured or killed by drunk drivers. But when I was young, it didn't seem like a big deal. Most people did it; it was how you got home from wherever you'd been partying. If you were lucky, nothing happened. Remember, we didn't have car seat belts then, or bike helmets either. The attitude was different.

One night during Pam's Calvin period, she called me and asked if I'd drive over to Cal's house and pick up her cardigan sweater. She'd left it there, was home with her mother, and didn't have an excuse to get out of the house. I called Cal to see if it was okay to come over, and he said yes. When I got to his place, I found a woman there with him. I started to get angry on Pam's behalf, but realized how ridiculous that was.

Calvin and his friend invited me to have a drink with them. I'd felt a cold coming on and had taken a Contac before I left my house. It was a new drug then, a long-acting capsule filled with revolutionary "tiny time pills." I'd never taken one before and had no idea that it could react with alcohol. The single gin-and-tonic made me so dizzy that Cal and his date ended up following me home to make sure I'd get there safely.

Courtesy of C. Linda Dowell

Allouez School, where our friendship started

The old railroad station in Green Bay has become a restaurant and microbrewery.

THE END, FOR A WHILE

You know the line about the fat lady. The overly *zaftig* diva belted her heart out during the last years of the sixties, and an era ended for four girls from Green Bay.

On January 12, 1969, I huddled under a cheap, newly-purchased quilt in a drafty apartment in Fremont, Ohio, listening on radio to Super Bowl III. The brash, upstart quarterback Joe Namath from the equally upstart American Football League was making good on his prediction that his New York Jets would beat the NFL's Baltimore Colts. Final score: Jets 16, Colts 7. The Packers under Phil Bengtson had finished 6–7–1 in the season just completed, good only for third place in the NFL's Central Division.

I had finished my college course work and come to Fremont to work as an announcer at WFRO Radio. There I learned some lessons about small-town living. Fremont was barely a third the size of Green Bay. Having been there all of ten days, I had no friends and few acquaintances. Scott was in the army at Fort Monmouth, New Jersey, and I pined for a weekend when I could see him. I felt chilled and completely alone.

The Packer team I knew was disintegrating. Paul Hornung had been picked up by New Orleans in their expansion draft in 1967. But hobbled by bad knees, he retired without playing a down for the Saints. Jim Taylor, a Louisiana native, played out his option in 1966, signed with the Saints, and carried the ball for them in '67 before he also retired. Mr. A had been traded, beginning an odyssey around the league. General manager Vince Lombardi, hoping to lead another team to the Super Bowl, left Green Bay to become head coach of the Washington Redskins in 1969. But on June 24, 1970, he was diagnosed with intestinal cancer, and on September 3 of that year he died. Bart Starr and Ray Nitschke extended their Packer careers into the seventies, but nothing was the same.

Soon after arriving in Fremont, I received a letter from Carla telling me that she was getting married, midway through her junior year in college. Within weeks of that news, Scott called to report his unexpected promotion to specialist fourth class. We had decided that when he made spec-four, we could be married. So I made a hasty exit from Fremont and went home to prepare for my own wedding. Both Scott and I would have preferred a quiet, civil ceremony, but my mother demurred. "Fine," I told her. "You plan whatever you want. I'll show up."

We took our vows on March 30, 1969, at the Ambassador East Hotel in Chicago, under a canopy of flowers, with an honest-to-God rabbi officiating and Pammy as my maid of honor. My mother had to organize the wedding hastily, working around Jewish holidays and Scott's leave from the army. "I was married at the Ambassador Hotel, and I wore a blue suit," she said. "Would you like to wear blue, too?"

"Mom!" I shrieked. "We're putting a wedding together in six weeks. If I wear blue, do you know what everybody's going to think?"

"Oooh, I hadn't thought of that. You'll wear white," my mother declared. And then, remembering a question she'd asked me, which I had answered truthfully *(it* was *the sixties!)*, she added, "Off-white." And so it was.

Pam was the next to wed, in a long, lacy dress of the pure white she'd earned, in an interminable Mass on a scorching day in August 1969 at old St. Willebrord's Church in downtown Green Bay. Since the church lacked air conditioning, and we knelt and rose so many times, the bride's cousin became faint and had to be taken outside by two groomsmen. I was an attendant, and Pam complained later that I'd spoiled her wedding photographs by not smiling. There were two reasons for my solemn demeanor. First, I believed she was rushing things. Her fiancé had recently returned from Vietnam and been discharged from the army. I didn't think they'd spent enough time together to be sure they were right for each other.

The second reason was this: She was welcoming her soldier boy back, but I was about to send mine off to that distant, deadly place. Scott had received his orders, and he left for 'Nam in October.

Del, the youngest by a few months, was the last of us to marry. Her ceremony in the early summer of 1970 was held outdoors and seemed to me vaguely hippieish. I hadn't seen her for a while, and I chuckled in surprise when our friend Cindy told me that not only was she keeping her maiden name, even her new husband did not presume to call her Dorothy.

And so the four of us were married, and set out into a chaotic world to take up our adult lives. And we all lived happily ever after.

Until ...

UNFINISHED BUSINESS

"I could have been Barbara Walters.
I could have been a TV star.
I could have been riding to my network job
In my fancy, chauffeured car.
Twenty years ago my classmates named me
The girl most likely to succeed.
But I didn't have enough ambition.
So I never got my life up to speed."

Ellen, "I Could Have Been Barbara Walters,"
Outtake from *Third and Long*

CRACKING WISE

I am learning to joke about getting old the way I learned to joke about cancer. Recently I was with a group of friends when the discussion turned to décolletage. "Cleavage?" a slender woman exclaimed. "I never had any!" And I heard myself pipe up, "I've always had it—but it's six inches lower than it used to be!"

There was a time when aging terrified me, and that's the theme of the next few chapters. But I brought up the subject of cancer, and this isn't one of those cancer memoirs, so let's get it out of the way.

In the fall of 2002, when I was diagnosed with breast cancer, I immediately thought of Fred "Fuzzy" Thurston. Fuzzy played guard for the Packers back in the glory days, and he lost his larynx to cancer in 1981. In 2002 (and in fact as I write), Fuzzy was still around, still greeting patrons at the bar he owned, still exhibiting an enormous zest for life. I decided his inspiration would get me through whatever was to come.

In *Distant Replay,* one of several books he wrote with Dick Schaap, Thurston's teammate Jerry Kramer told a story in which Fuzzy went out to play golf with some Packer buddies shortly after his surgery. "You got to give me three strokes a side for cancer," Fuzzy directed his friends.

"How could he say that?" I wondered. *"How could anyone ever say something like that?"* That quotation stuck in my mind for years.

And then came the day when I'd had my lumpectomy, finished chemo, started radiation, and come up with a lot of bald jokes plus some other humor that's too black to repeat. I was on my way to a radiation appointment when a policeman pulled me over. I looked him square in the eye and said, "Sorry I was speeding, officer, but I'm late for my cancer treatment."

He took note of my head, filmed with hair a quarter-inch long, and let me go with a warning to be careful.

I relished telling all of my friends the story of how I beat the traffic ticket. But the best part was that I ran into Fuzzy at Eve's a year later and was able to share it with him. He responded with a big grin and a hug.

Cancer can often be cured, and so far I've been lucky. There's no cure for aging. But I'm handling it far better than I did on a certain unseasonably cool morning in 1984. I went a little bit crazy that day.

A MOST PECULIAR
MID-LIFE CRISIS

Blame it on the jet stream. The dippy thing took a dive, early in that summer of '84, and steamy, sultry Cincinnati was transformed. I opened my window and shut my eyes, and suddenly I was breathing the bracing air of Wisconsin. And not just Wisconsin, but the Green Bay, Wisconsin, of my youth. As the chilly breeze and the memories flooded over me, a most peculiar stage in my life got started. And so did a play called *Third and Long*.

The summer before, I had left a job I'd held for ten years, writing sales promotion copy for *U.S. News & World Report* magazine in Washington, DC, to follow my husband to Cincinnati, Ohio. It was a given in those days that I would go wherever my husband's career took him, and I was honestly thrilled to leave the yuppified East Coast for the Midwest where I'd grown up. On my first visit to the Queen City, I spotted two old women in fifties-style housedresses exiting a store that I was about to enter. They so resembled Frances—the housekeeper who had cared for me as a child—that I immediately fell in love with my future home.

I have never seen women like them since, in Cincinnati or anywhere else. But the deal was done.

Any psychology student could tell you I was ripe for emotional crisis. The move was far from the only thing that had caused upheaval in my life. Between 1977 and 1983 I had birthed a son, lost my mother and both paternal grandparents, inherited money, quit a job, and moved a third of the way across the country to take up life as a stay-at-home mom. But what unsettled me the most was that in the fall of 1982, I passed my thirty-fifth birthday.

At *U.S. News,* we based our sales presentations on demographics—statistics of age, gender, education, income, and the like. We spent a lot of time talking about young people—defined as age eighteen to thirty-four. At that time, eighteen to thirty-four meant the baby boomers. There were so many of us, it was "in" to be young. But now I was thirty-five, which was uncomfortably close to forty. By definition, I was no longer young. And when a woman realizes that she's no longer young, it can be an occasion for depression or panic.

For me it was panic. And my panic increased when I visited my parents, picked up the *Press-Gazette,* and saw a byline that unnerved me. I'd feuded with a certain boy from nursery school through high school. We'd been notorious for hating each other so long that I couldn't even remember why. And there was his name on the sports page. Cliff Christl was a reporter on the Packer beat.

That's right. My old nemesis—who didn't even work for the high school paper I edited—now had my dream job. What's more, my dad (fairly or unfairly) told me that he thought Cliff's critical reporting had spurred the firing of Bart Starr from the Packers' head-coaching position. Starr the paragon, the seventeenth-round draft choice out of Alabama who made it to the Hall of Fame, the wholesome husband and father who played quarterback for the Packers for so many years and set so many records. I admit his coaching record, 52–76–3, was hardly stellar. But this was like ... dissing Jesus.

(Cliff moved up to the *Milwaukee Journal-Sentinel,* where he was regarded as a Packer guru by the time he retired at age sixty. Today he writes books about the Packers and contributes columns to both papers. His writing about the old days is knowledgeable and entertaining. We finally spoke cordially at our forty-year class reunion in 2005.)

Speaking of reunions, I had another unsettling experience at my twenty-five-year reunion in 1990. Fortunately I was over the age/panic thing by that time, or it could have been devastating. A classmate asked me what I was doing, and I replied that I was doing some volunteer work and a bit of freelance writing. Before he could control himself, his face crumpled and he blurted out, *"Oh, no!"* I had begun to feel better about my life, so I took it in stride. But I knew where this guy—I'll call him Jack—was coming from.

Jack had worked very hard for everything he had. He grew up in modest circumstances. But he focused his entire high school career on getting into a military academy, and he made it. He took advantage of every opportunity the service had to offer him, and when I saw him at that reunion, he had become not only a high-ranking officer, but also a medical doctor. Although my admiration for Jack is boundless, I have to say that my lifestyle is absolutely none of his business. But you can see what his expectations were.

Jack couldn't envision me, class salutatorian, news editor of the paper, with everything made easy for me, becoming—as protagonist Ellen describes herself in *Third and Long*—"a small-time, part-time, freelance writer." And a few years earlier, neither could I.

More disturbing was something my friend Joan said when she came to visit shortly after I moved from DC to Cincinnati. I was excited to host Joan and her family, and I pulled out all the stops. Enamored of my new home, I offered my guests Cincinnati delicacies—Graeter's ice cream, Skyline chili, mettwurst—and insisted they try everything. I baked pizza from scratch and didn't even freak when Joan's daughter dropped a piece cheese-side-down on my shag carpeting. I chauffeured my friends around the city, pointing out sights of interest. I thought I'd been a great hostess.

But Joan told me, "You're working too hard. This isn't fun for you or for us. You're turning into a regular Jewish mother."

I supposed Joan—née Goldberg—ought to know one when she saw one. Was she right? Was I turning into a Jewish mother, like *my* mother, like my *mother-in-law*? Even worse, was I turning into a

guilt-inducing ...

Q: How many Jewish mothers does it take to change a light bulb?
A. Never mind, I'll sit in the dark.

... food-pushing ...

Story of every Jewish holiday: They tried to kill us; we won; let's eat.

... chronically anxious ...

Jewish telegram: "Begin worrying. Details to follow."

... Jewish mother JOKE?

Was *this* the image I wanted for my middle years?

By the summer of '84, my unsettled feelings had blossomed into a true mid-life crisis. It seems silly now, looking back from past sixty, but I became obsessed with age. I was obnoxious, asking people how old they were and trying to judge whether they looked younger for their age than I did. I began to dwell on—and regret—the life choices I'd made.

And because the Packers had been so woven into my earlier life, football became part of my obsession. Turning thirty-seven in 1984, I was older than just about every player in the National Football League. And what had I accomplished?

I began to see my girlhood as an idyll. And to make matters worse, I couldn't stop thinking about Mr. A. One day I grabbed a book at random, and it was his memoir from the seventies. I ended up re-reading the whole thing, and I began to worry. The book told me that Mr. A had become a rebel; he wasn't the Jolly Green Giant anymore. What was going on with him after all these years? Was he all right? If he wasn't, could I help him? I became fixated, but I didn't know how to find him.

But as stressed-out as I was, I could see the humor in what was happening to me. And so ... **I turned my mid-life crisis into a musical comedy.**

CREATING *THIRD AND LONG*

ELLEN:

I can't believe this. Every time I look in a mirror, I do a double-take …"Mom, what are you doing here?" And that's not even the worst. It just hit me, a few weeks ago. I'm older than almost every player in the National Football League.

JUDY *(PUZZLED)*:

Yeah?

ELLEN:

And … I've … never … slept … with one of them!

JUDY:

Umm … I'm not following this.

ELLEN:

Don't you see? I'm so old, now I'll never get to.

JUDY:

That's your big problem? What is this, mid-life crisis or second childhood?

I hadn't thought much about football in the years between Green Bay and Cincinnati, and I don't believe my friends had either. Except for Carla, who remained in Wisconsin, we rarely could see Packer games on TV. We were preoccupied with establishing our careers, rearing our children, and conforming (or not) to our husbands' expectations. But now I wasn't working, and my only child was in school. I had too much time to think. And time to write.

So my response to all the *tsuris* in my life was to start writing *Third and Long*—a musical comedy about a Jewish mother, a retired football player, and their unfinished business. I distilled all of my fond memories and my disturbing new feelings into the script, spending as much time as I could in my fantasy world. When I gave my husband a "Not tonight, honey," so I could plot out a fictional union instead, I knew I was in a bad way.

ELLEN *(SINGS)*:

I was the first in my family
To go to college.
I made a three-point average.
I met a guy.
I've realized my concrete expectations.
But those old fantasies … the crazy ones … won't die.

We had a program to follow.
It all seemed perfect.
House in a classy suburb,
Two jobs, two cars.
A cat and then a son made us a family.
I never dared to dream that more was in the stars. …

If life's a journey, this moment
Should be a crossroad.
Well, it's a dead end, rather.
I don't know why
I can't stop thinking I'm midway to nowhere.
I want to soar, but I've forgotten how to fly.

Mid-life … mid-life … mid-life crisis …
Mid-life crisis creeping up on me.

Set in the summer and fall of 1985, *Third and Long* tells the story of Ellen Rosenthal, who's nearing her thirty-eighth birthday and is definitely not enjoying it. She's afraid she's turning into a Jewish mother—specifically *her* mother. Ellen has everything she thought she wanted, but she isn't satisfied. Her lawyer husband, Dave, provides well for her. He may not pay her the rapt attention he used to, but at least he's faithful. And she dotes on her little son. But her own career is stagnant, and instead of fixing that, she's spending her time thinking about Rick Rokowski, the pro football player she adored in her youth.

ELLEN *(SINGS)*:

Do you favor caution
Or enjoy a dare?
Do you think it's funny
That I still might care?

What's happened since we parted long ago?
It's none of my business, but I'd like to know.

When Ellen tells her friend Judy about her preoccupation with Rick, Judy tries to cheer her up.

JUDY *(SINGS):*

When the going gets tough, the tough go shopping.
There's no time for stopping when life treats you rough.
Though your dream's gone stale and balloons are popping,
And it seems like the whole world's calling your bluff,
If you're strong enough, you'll skim off the topping.
The tough go shopping … when the going gets tough.

But when Ellen says that approach won't work, Judy surprises her by suggesting, "Maybe ... you know, just one glorious night. If no one gets hurt, and you feel better ..."

Ellen returns to her hometown, a thinly-disguised Green Bay, for her twenty-year class reunion. There, she meets up with Rick—cutely and expediently, as people in musical comedies do. He takes her to the tavern owned by super-fan Barney. There, in a back room crammed with football memorabilia, they encounter their team's current quarterback, the impossibly perfect John.

JOHN:
The most fun thing in life is proving you can do something nobody thought you could. I do it every Sunday.

Sneaking into the tavern is sixteen-year-old Michelle, a football groupie who does all of the things Ellen did at her age (even her name is intended as an echo). She tells John some things that I never got a chance to say to Mr. A:

MICHELLE:
I'm not ready to go to bed with anyone, and I'm certainly not looking to get married. ... I just want to mean something to you. I want to be part of this legend you're building.

Rounding out the cast is Taylor, a sportscaster who was Ellen's high-school classmate. For spite, I made this character conceited and one-dimensional. *Take that, Cliff Christl!*

Ellen tries to connect with Rick, but finds that he is having mid-life issues of his own. When she suggests, in inevitable Jewish-mother style, that she'd like to take care of him, he rebels.

RICK *(SINGS)*:
I'm telling you straight, and it's making you frantic.
You're trapped in the past, and you're far too romantic.

Your surge of emotion is way out of place.
Now give me some freedom, and give me some space! …

You're in love with some words that a sportswriter penned.
I'm not your fiancé, or even your friend.
Got that? Period! The End!

Ellen reacts physically to this, almost as though Rick is striking her. But *Third and Long* is a musical comedy, and besides, it's my own romantic fantasy. It has to have a happy ending. It's John who comes to Ellen's rescue. Turns out he has a surprising predilection for Jewish mothers. Oh yeah, and food comes into that, too.

JOHN *(SINGS)*:
Everyone should have a Jewish mother.
It's her cooking that will really fill the bill.
I'll never fear the blitzing of a defense out to kill.
I'll never see a trainer and I'll never pop a pill
For she'll have something delicious that'll cure my every ill—
Everyone should have a Jewish mother.

Audience members are left to make up their own minds as to whether Ellen gets to experience her "one glorious night." The next day, she plays a role in her team's victory. Ellen's weekend does not turn out as she expected. But when it is over, she not only has made up with Rick, she's ready to return home with a new self-image and a determination to make her life work out.

ELLEN:
This incredible weekend! The highs and the lows—I'm feeling things I haven't felt in years. I feel so alive! I found out I can make things happen! I made something happen today, didn't I? Not bad for an old broad.

RICK:

Not bad, period.

* * *

The first people to read *Third and Long* were a couple about my age. I'll call them Julie and Jerry. They brought their children to the drama class that my son attended. I'd bring the new pages and we'd hang out in the school cafeteria to read and discuss them till the kids were ready to leave. What makes this significant is that Julie and Jerry were each married to someone else when we started, and a couple of years later they were together. It would be presumptuous to think that *Third and Long* had anything to do with this. But it's reasonable to say that Julie and Jerry were questioning their lives in the same way that I was. In a sense, we validated each other.

* * *

A strange thing happened while I was writing the show. Late in the summer of '84, I was on a plane between Cincinnati and DC, going to visit my former employer, *U.S. News & World Report*. I was carrying an early draft of *Third and Long* to show to my copywriter friends. This manuscript included the lyrics for "None of My Business," the ballad Ellen sings to the absent Rick.

We made a stop in Mr. A's hometown. A tall man wearing a Stetson hat and cowboy boots boarded the plane. He looked like my old hero, minus a little weight and a lot of hair. I had read an anecdote about a Stetson and boots in Mr. A's book. Could this be he? *Had I willed him into being there?* I wanted to talk to my fellow passenger, but we hit some turbulence and had to stay in our seats.

At the baggage claim, I danced around the tall fellow, afraid to speak, looking in vain for luggage with initials. I flashed him a smile, figuring he'd return it and maybe his smile would knock me over as it had in the old days. He did. And it didn't. (But then, a decade in the trenches of the

NFL isn't exactly smile-enhancing. It still could have been Mr. A.) Finally I told myself that the mature thing to do was to let him walk away. So … he picked up his suitcase and walked away.

Maturely I said to myself, *"AAAARGH!"* And I obsessed about that encounter for the next two years.

I have never seen Mr. A since that day, if indeed it was he in the airport. My son shares his name, but that is entirely by coincidence—although my own mother asked me about it when the boy was born. I turned that into a running gag in *Third and Long;* Ellen repeatedly insists that her son, Ricky, is not named after Rick Rokowski. If you don't believe me or Ellen, consider this: Carla gave one of her sons the same name as her childhood dog. Sometimes you just like the name.

* * *

I worked on the script, off and on, for four years, searching fruitlessly for someone to write music for my lyrics. I adore musical comedy, but there was no way I could come up with the melodies myself. I had seven years of piano lessons when I was a kid, but I can't play a simple tune. Frankly, I'm almost tone-deaf.

I joined a playwrights' group and hooked up with two young men who needed someone to write dialogue for *their* musical. I contributed a naughty—and frankly, forgettable—book. We participated in a festival held at Cincinnati Playhouse in the Park and then did a month in an improvised cabaret. But when it came time to return the favor, the guys declined to score my show.

I found two more composers through the writers' group and worked with them for a year. They wrote some tunes in their spare time, but then said they had more pressing projects and couldn't continue. When I asked for the sheet music they had already written, they informed me, "We're jingle writers. Jingle writers don't write things down." So I had nothing to show for that year.

By now I was getting used to being "old," my topical references had lost their freshness, and I too needed to move on, so *Third and Long* went on the shelf. But the years and the satisfaction of creating something had cooled my frustrations. I felt almost as if I had lived through Ellen's adventure and learned the lessons she learned. Eventually my fiftieth birthday came along, and then my sixtieth—with none of the angst I felt at forty.

Even today, though, I find myself—in the shower or behind the wheel of my car—singing *Third and Long* lyrics to artless tunes of my own invention. Ellen, Rick, Michelle, and the others are still very real to me. One objective in writing this book was to give them life again.

* * *

Something I learned from the whole experience is that although I thought I had reinvented myself several times, I was still basically the same person I was during my high-school years. I'd lived in a lot of different places, gotten away from football for a while, but now I was feeling almost the same impulses and emotions that I did as a girl in the sixties.

I was ready to reconnect with my friends from Green Bay, although it would be another decade before we would all come together.

Press-Gazette Collection of the Neville Public Museum of Brown County

I've mentioned my father's interest in acting, and his collection of theater books. Of course, these were influences on my writing *Third and Long*. In the fall of 1977, following the death of former Green Bay Community Theater president Katie Cott, my father offered his collection of 318 books to CT as a memorial to his friend Mrs. Cott. Community Theater officials then donated the books—adding more than fifty scripts of their own—to the Brown County Library, where they would be more accessible to the public. This *Press-Gazette* photo from January 7, 1978, shows my father, Sidney Shaw, looking over the books with Mildred Lorberblatt, head of the library's history, literature, and social sciences department. At the time, this was the largest individual book donation ever given to the library.

BITTERSWEET

After my mother's death in 1979, my father began dating a succession of women who all seemed to be around my age. Instead of resenting this, I was happy that he had the companionship and didn't require more from me than I could give while I was hundreds of miles away, holding a job and caring for a small child.

Dad, his friends (whose names have been changed), and I turned into a weird, quasi-family unit. When I visited Green Bay, Claire "did my colors" and sold me beauty products. Gayle brought her son to play with mine. I was perhaps most comfortable with Angela, who'd graduated from East High two years before me. Sometimes I'd leave my boy with his Poppa while Angie and I went out for dinner or drinks. I learned that Angie had fantasies about the Packers, too. I saw her face fall when I mentioned one day that the popular tight end, Paul Coffman, had gotten married.

One night in the mid-eighties, Angie and I went to a restaurant that Fuzzy Thurston operated on the West Side. This was a bigger place than the taverns Fuzzy has owned since, a supper club with a full menu. They had a great Steak Diane, prepared tableside; not a classic Diane but ... *enough with the food already!* After dinner, Angie and I moved to the bar where Fuzzy sat with some other patrons. Someone put Mary Hopkin's "Those Were the Days" on the jukebox and we all sang along with feeling:

"Those were the days, my friend. We thought they'd never end..."

That was a bittersweet moment, being there with Fuzzy, singing those words, and recalling the long-gone Lombardi days. I was deeply into writing *Third and Long* and figured I'd live out my fantasy just a bit. I don't remember exactly what I said to Fuzzy, but it was something about being a Jewish mother.

The only problem was that it was noisy in the place, and Fuzzy couldn't hear me properly. "I had a Jewish lover once," he replied, giving me an affectionate pat.

Another time, Angie introduced me to a friend of hers who'd dated a Packer player toward the end of the Lombardi era. This woman—I'll call her Lois—had been a dancer at The Tropics, a club that succeeded Speed's as a player hangout. I'm sure she was lithe and lovely then, but when I met her, she was plain, plump, and forty. Our conversation turned to a recent reunion of the first Super Bowl team. I asked Lois whether she'd seen her old friend when he was in town. "No," she replied, her slumping shoulders indicating how impossible it would be to take up where they'd left off. "But when they interviewed him on TV, he asked if The Tropics was still open. And I knew he was thinking of me."

I'M LUCKY, I GUESS

Somehow my marriage survived the *Third and Long* phase. In fact, among the four friends, I'm the only one married to her original husband, and I occasionally wonder why. "Inertia," Scott and I like to explain, but there has to be more to it than that. *There's love there; you just don't always see it at first glance.* I don't believe Scott and I are smarter, or more persevering, or more pliant than my friends and their spouses. I guess we're just luckier.

I've already mentioned that Del's husband left her (after twenty-one years and three kids) for a woman he met in China. As for Pam, she and her first husband—I'll call him Glenn—were living in Louisiana and expecting a baby when he abruptly informed her that he didn't want the responsibility of being a husband and father. He moved out almost immediately after their son was born. Pam, the scrupulous Catholic, was able to get their marriage annulled on the grounds that Glenn did not enter into it in good faith.

During the difficult time that followed, Nathalie, the principal of the school where Pam taught, became a mentor to her. And eventually Nathalie introduced Pam to her son, Andre. It was not long before they were married. Andre adopted Pam's little boy, and they've had two daughters together.

Glenn did not stay in touch with Pam, but I had a weird encounter with him at National Airport in Washington, DC, a few years later. Scott and I were there to pick up my father, who had come to visit us. Dad looked across the terminal and said, "Isn't that …" Before I could stop him, he called out a greeting and started over to Glenn. Under these awkward circumstances, Glenn was obliged to ask me what I had heard from Pam. I pulled out my wallet and showed him a photo of his son, whom he hadn't seen since the boy was a few days old. It seemed incredible that I should possess this picture, while he did not. And then, suffused with embarrassment but compelled to set the record straight, I showed Glenn another photo—this one of Pam and Andre's first, tiny daughter.

Pam and I both thought Glenn might contact her after this meeting, but he didn't. In fairness to him, he may have felt he would be in her way. But I wonder whether it ever enters his mind that his son—now in his midthirties—might still be searching for him.

I've long had regrets about a time when I feel I should have been there for Carla but wasn't. She married while in college and had a baby right away. Still, she got her degree on schedule and supported her husband through dental school. A few years later, I received a letter addressed to me in Carla's looping backhand. The contents shocked me. Carla had been seeing a former boyfriend and wanted to leave her husband for him. But before they could act on their plans, the young man, a pilot, was killed in a crash. I sent condolences, but I also wrote some platitudes about appreciating what she did have, the dentist and their daughter. I was in Greensboro, North Carolina then, thrilled to have my own husband safely back from Vietnam and out of the army, thankful that we finally had the ability to take charge of our own lives. A devastating thing had happened to my friend, but I couldn't see beyond the place where I was to comfort her properly.

Years later when I received another letter—Carla was going to marry her boss—my reaction was more appropriate. This was to be her third marriage; her prospective husband was older and had been married long enough to have grown children. Some of their friends dropped them. We didn't. And as it turns out, I like her current husband the best of the three. Even though he is a Bear fan.

By that time I had gained enough maturity to see that there isn't one set of rules for everybody. You do what you have to do, and you base it on what you know and feel at the time. It may be the right thing or the wrong thing, because you can't always foresee the consequences. But there's no point in judging someone else's actions unless they deliberately set out to hurt someone. And that was never Carla's intent. When I see her now, she seems happy, and I fervently hope that she is.

QUEST FOR COMPLETION

"I've spent a lifetime
Taking a back seat.
Learning to act sweet,
Shy and sincere.
Some chose the fast lane.
I've always kept out.
Now this girl's stepped out.
My chance is here.

'Cause it's my turn now.
I can make things right somehow.
Tellin' you, it's my turn, my turn now."

Ellen, "My Turn Now," closing number,
Third and Long

THIS CHAPTER HAS A TEN-YEAR STATUTE OF LIMITATIONS!

My security-conscious husband is not to know about this incident until at least ten years after it happened, which will be September 23, 2017. If you know my husband, do not tell him. If you are skimming this volume in a bookstore in Cincinnati prior to 9/23/17, and you see a large, bespectacled, gray-bearded man turning to this chapter, kindly snatch the book out of his hands. I AM COMPLETELY SERIOUS.

Sunday morning, September 23, 2007. The sky is blue; the sun is bright. The air is full of autumn crispness and promise and probably a bit of paper-mill effluvium, since we are, after all, in Green Bay. The Packers are 2–0, and they play the San Diego Chargers this afternoon. Nobody really expects them to have an undefeated season, but it is still mathematically possible, so all of fandom is in a good mood. There was a parade yesterday, to honor the fiftieth anniversary of Lambeau Field. It was a clunky, but charming, little home-grown parade with vintage cars and vintage players, including Bart Starr, Paul Hornung, and Max McGee. It had high school bands, cheerleading students from a local academy, and (I think) a couple of the original Golden Girls cheerleaders from the sixties. It was totally Green Bay. It was totally perfect.

Pam and I come out of the Days Inn–Lambeau Field at about quarter to eight in the morning. As is our custom, I'm driving her to Mass before the game. As I locate my car, I recall that I had a spot of trouble parking it last night. The lot was almost full. As I attempted to pull out and re-enter at the far end of the lot, I almost hit a sawhorse that was blocking the exit. I hadn't had much to drink and my night vision is still fair, but the sawhorse was painted Packer green and was difficult to see in the dark. Another sawhorse was sitting in a perfectly good parking space. Del and Carla jumped out of the car and moved the obstruction so I could park. A group of revelers, sitting on the ground in the corner of the lot, were yelling at me, but I ignored them. I had my Days Inn parking pass on my dashboard, so I had a right to be there.

As I approach my car in the morning light, my first impression is that someone is playing a practical joke on me. A figure is draped over my steering wheel, a small man in a plaid shirt. I suddenly realize that *this is not a dummy, ohmigod, this is a real man,* and in all the confusion I obviously forgot to lock my car last night. I rap on the window and the man raises his head. I am so relieved that he is not dead that I don't scream, I don't call 911, I simply open the door and announce, "This is my car."

"Oh, okay," he says politely. He climbs out and strolls away. I check the car. Nothing has been taken and nothing extraneous left behind except a pervasive odor of alcohol.

Pam and I roll down the windows and continue on to Nativity of Our Lord Church on Oneida Street. It is Game Day Morning, and all is right with the world.

FOR THE LOVE OF ...

When we were about fifteen, something happened between Carla and me that threatened to terminate our friendship. At the time, it seemed too risky for discussion, and I only learned the truth of it decades later.

Carla and I were riding the bus home from school one day. Back then, high school students didn't use backpacks like the kids tote around now. Most of us carried our books in our arms, in a stack. Typically this was anchored by a hefty loose-leaf notebook, filled with dividers for our various subjects. Piled on the notebook were our textbooks, and finally the girls would tuck a little clutch purse against our chests, on top.

The bus got to Arrowhead Drive before it arrived at my stop, but Carla stayed on. The route went south on Webster Avenue, then west near the De Pere line, toward the river. At Riverside Drive, the bus would turn north, passing Arrowhead again as it headed back downtown. Since Carla and Del both lived closer to the bottom of their street, they often preferred to wait and walk from that end, especially if it was cold or raining. I got off in front of my house on Webster, went in, put my books down, and realized that my purse was missing.

I phoned my friends, and my parents called the bus company, but no one came up with my purse. It was annoying and a little scary, but not catastrophic. I didn't have a driver's license yet. I didn't even carry keys, since my dad, the erstwhile New Yorker, found it brag-worthy that we never locked the back door to our house. My indulgent parents didn't punish me for my carelessness, but replaced the purse, my wallet, and the little bit of cash I carried. With a new library card and student ID, I was back in business.

At least a month went by, maybe two. I was home one afternoon when Carla called and asked if she and her mother could stop by. *Her mother?* Carla's voice was somber, without its usual mischievous lilt. I told her to come over, and I began to panic.

I had just read John Knowles' *A Separate Peace,* a novel about boys at a prep school during World War II. The book was not yet considered a classic and taught in schools as it is today. I had never heard of it and had found it by accident at the library, but when I closed the cover on it, I cradled it in my hands like treasure. To me, Knowles' views on violence were less interesting than the relationship between the narrator, Gene, and his daring friend Phineas. They reminded me of myself and Carla. It hit me hard when, at the end of the novel, Phineas died. So, as I waited for the Porters' station wagon to pull up in my driveway, I fancied that Carla and her mother were coming to break the news that my friend was terminally ill. Maybe she had leukemia, or a leaky heart valve. I envisioned her growing pale and weak, no longer able to outshine all the rest of us at running, passing, and kicking. I was terrified, thinking that all we had enjoyed together in the past two years was coming to an end.

The car arrived. Carla and her mother got out, their faces grim. I ran to the door, breathless, and threw it open. For a moment, no one said anything.

Then, "Well?" Mrs. Porter demanded. Carla took her arms from behind her back and handed me … **my purse.**

I was so shocked that I could only stammer, "Thank you. What … uh … what …?"

"Come on," Mrs. Porter said to her daughter, and marched her back to the car.

Carla and I went about our usual routines after that, and neither of us spoke of the incident. I had my purse back and she wasn't dying, so what did we have to say? I had so idolized Carla that it pained me to see her chastened, and I refused to see myself as her victim. But as I put this book together, I remembered that day, and at last I had the courage to ask her what had happened.

I e-mailed my friend of almost fifty years, "I never knew why you did that. Were you angry at me about something? Did you want to have a piece of me to hold onto? Were you afraid I'd think you stole it in the first place? *Did* you steal it in the first place? And if so, why?"

Carla's reply, when I got it, almost put me on the floor.

"Here is what I remember," she wrote. "I had every intention of calling you as soon as I got home. But I remembered you had some piece of paper on which Paul Hornung had written, 'Love, Paul,' in your wallet. I was very infatuated with Paul Hornung at that time (as you were) and wanted to pretend for awhile that it had been written to me. I remember that my mother found your purse in my closet, and you know the rest. Thanks for not hating me over that. I was just being immature."

I've acquired several Hornung autographs since that time, and I cherish them, but it's funny, I'd forgotten I ever had that piece of paper. I wonder what happened to it.

"I NEED AN ENDING
FOR MY STORY!"

"Can't wait, can't wait." My friends and I have been e-mailing for weeks. Our 2010 trip is especially important, because we didn't make one last year and a predicted labor dispute threatens the 2011 season.

I scored a bonus trip this year. Six weeks before our Packer date, I drove to Green Bay to attend my forty-five-year high school reunion. Conditioned to Cincinnati's hills, my eyes feasted on the glorious flatness, the neat geometrics that defined the boundaries of my youth. I know I couldn't reside here full-time—I'm not the same person I was, I've lived too many other places and done too many things—but I still love to walk the familiar terrain every chance I get.

The reunion was pleasant, although there were few Allouez people on hand. My main impression was that far too many people were talking about their "bucket lists." *We don't need to go there yet, do we?*

Sometimes, though, I do reflect on my own mortality. A surprising number of people have asked me whether I'd like to have my ashes scattered at Lambeau Field. You know, there's an ordinance up there—you can't do that. Too many people would take advantage. It would be kind of icky for the players, I guess.

But I've told my son I wouldn't mind if he brought my ashes home some day, maybe to a beautiful, secluded spot along the great sweep of the bay. *Not too close to the paper mill, dear.*

This year's trip has an added dimension for me. I'm determined to finish this book, so it's not just a vacation; it's a working trip. I'm hoping something will present itself during this journey—a telling anecdote, a wise summation—that will provide a definitive ending. I'm on a quest for completion.

At Northwestern in the sixties we studied a film style called *cinema verité*. This genre made use of small, hand-held cameras that had recently been developed. The filmmaker would take his camera into a real-life situation and record it as unobtrusively as possible. The objective was to present "film truth," as opposed to a story that started with a script. I always took the position that it wasn't possible to achieve absolute truth, since the very presence of the filmmaker altered the situation. Now I'm hoping that my taking notes throughout our stay won't alter the situation and spoil the fun for my friends.

But when we gather at Green Bay's Cambria Suites *(nice hotel, dinky pool)* on Friday night, there doesn't seem to be a problem. We fall easily into conversation, as if we've never been apart. We always do.

Pam is venting about her husband, who recently retired. Now that he's home a lot, he makes her account to him for her activities, report where she's going every time she leaves the house. Of course, it never occurs to him to do the same. He brought home all the personal belongings from his office, but he hasn't unpacked them and they're sitting around in boxes.

While Pam is chafing at too much togetherness, Del is looking for more. Still our only single member, she has exciting news. During Door County summers in 1966 and '67, she briefly dated a boy I'll call Todd. She lost track of him, but a few years ago she received an e-mail: *"I've been looking for you for years!"* Recently they've been e-mailing regularly, and Todd will pick her up at the conclusion of our stay, at Carla's family cottage in Sturgeon Bay. They'll spend a few days in Sister Bay, a little farther up the peninsula. We are both elated and terrified for her.

Saturday morning we head to the Packers Pro Shop at Lambeau Field. It is Alumni Weekend, and the Pro Shop has set up a table for player appearances. Pam is browsing near the table, glancing at a photograph, when she hears a voice behind her, "That's the handsomest man who ever played for the Packers!" She turns around, and there is my father's old friend, Lew Carpenter. It's his picture, of course, and he's scheduled to sign autographs along with seventies star Steve Odom. At seventy-eight, Lew appears frail, but he still has a big grin and a twinkle in his eye. He professes to remember us and envelops us in hugs.

(Carpenter was never a major NFL star, but his value to his teams—Detroit, then Cleveland, and finally the Packers—was immeasurable because he was so versatile. He could play halfback, fullback, end, and defensive back. He returned punts, and he undoubtedly could have gone in at quarterback if his team had needed him there. After his playing career ended, Lew served as an assistant coach for the Packers under two former teammates, head coaches Bart Starr and Forrest Gregg. He passed away about two months after we saw him, on November 14, 2010.)

Another alumnus, Jim Taylor, is scheduled to autograph his new book, *The Fire Within,* at three o'clock. Now, Taylor has always been Del's guy. While Carla and I sighed over the flashy, multitalented Hornung, Del preferred the relentless, straightforward running style and rugged good looks of Paul's backfield mate. "I don't know if I'll buy a book," she tells me now, "but I'd like to get a look at him!"

The signing is hours away, so we head out from the Pro Shop. We drive up and down Oneida Street, but we can't find one of our favorite souvenir shops. We have lunch at Kroll's, and the cashier there tells us the shop moved. But when we go to the street she mentions, the shop is not there. Finally the proprietor of a competing store tells us that our shop went out of business. "They just couldn't make it," he relates. "Receipts fell eighty-five percent when Brett Favre left town. I thought it was just me, but then I saw a statement from the Pro Shop, and theirs was the same."

We realize that the town is still bitterly divided over the Favre incident. Exactly what's supposed to have happened depends on who's telling the story, but some facts are indisputable. Brett Favre was quarterback of the Packers from 1992 through 2007. He broke most of Bart Starr's passing records, set a new league mark for consecutive starts, and led the Pack to two Super Bowls, one of which they won. He was named most valuable player in the NFL in 1995, '96, and '97. He played with the enthusiasm of a little boy, and although he earned millions, he made fans believe that he would play for nothing if he had to, just for love of the game. He's number twenty on the NFL Network's list of the top one hundred players of all time.

After the 2007 season, Favre retired, saying in a tearful speech that he had nothing left to give. A few months later he changed his mind, but the Packers—headed by general manager Ted Thompson and Coach Mike McCarthy—had moved on. They had groomed Aaron Rodgers to succeed Favre and felt that he was ready. Favre then expressed a desire to play for the Minnesota Vikings, who seemed to have all the pieces of a championship team except a top-echelon quarterback. But the Packers management wasn't about to let him go to a team in the same division. Instead, they traded him to the New York Jets.

Favre spent the 2008 season with the Jets and retired again at the end of that season. He asked the Jets to release him from all contractual obligations, and when they did, he came back from retirement again and signed with the Vikings. Since that time, every Packers–Vikings meeting has been billed as a grudge match.

Some people will tell you that Favre was a diva who was distant from the younger players and put his own interests ahead of the team. They say he had to go. Others insist that Thompson and McCarthy committed an egregious sin, alienating a hero and allowing a treasure to slip through their hands. Both sides agree that the situation was handled badly.

The struggling shopkeeper will speak no ill of Favre. "Brett is a good guy, and he loves Wisconsin," he tells us. "He still gives two million dollars a year to Wisconsin charities."

By this time, the Taylor signing is well underway, so we head back to the Pro Shop. "Let's just see how long the line is," I suggest. We discover that the line is very short indeed—because the Pro Shop has sold out of Jim's book. And Taylor's agreement dictates that he will sign only books.

I look at Del, and I can see in her face that she desperately wants that autographed book. And I've promised to pick one up for Jarreth's mother, Jean. "I can run down to Shopko," I say. "They had a whole table of books this morning."

"You won't have time!" Del protests.

But the thing about Green Bay is that even today, you can get pretty much wherever you want in fifteen minutes or less. Taylor is scheduled to be there for another forty-five minutes. "I can do it," I tell her. I turn and jog purposefully out to the parking lot, imagining I'm Taylor heading for the end zone.

As I near the Bay Park Square shopping center where Shopko is located, my cell phone chimes. "Can you get four copies?" Del asks. "The guy behind me in line wants two."

I'm just pulling into a parking space when the phone chimes again. "Six!" is all Del has to say.

I race into the store and find the table still half-full of books. I grab six and check myself out. I call Del back. "Got 'em. Don't let Jim leave!"

I re-enter the Pro Shop to a chorus of cheers. I feel as if I've crossed the goal line. I have only the six copies, but I could easily have unloaded two dozen. A woman with a young son has reserved copies five and six. "You made our day," she tells me.

All right, it's a cute story; it features an old-time player, but it's hardly definitive. This isn't my ending.

On Sunday we watch the Packers beat the Buffalo Bills, 34–7. The returning alumni are introduced at halftime. We feel a pang of regret that Ron Kramer is not among them. Kramer, who defined the tight-end position on Vince Lombardi's teams, died eight days earlier at the age of seventy-five. *Another one lost.* Bart Starr is there and is introduced last. As always, the loudest cheers are reserved for him.

Mr. A does not attend, and this disappoints me. I'm not yearning to see him, but our reunion would have provided a neat and natural conclusion to the book. *Don't get the wrong idea. That fire is out.*

When the contest is over, we return to our hotel for drinks, snacks, and a later game on TV. After a while, Carla says, "Let's go back to the stadium and see what's going on." Pam doesn't enjoy walking, and Del wants to catch up on e-mail, but I'm ready.

Carla and I head down Tony Canadeo Run to Brett Favre Pass, streets that didn't exist in our youth. As we reach Holmgren Way—named for

Mike Holmgren, the head coach who took the Packers to Super Bowls XXXI and XXXII—we meet a couple heading in the other direction. The husband is wearing Packer green and gold, while the wife is in full Chicago Bears regalia. Carla banters with them about mate-swapping.

We hike around the huge bowl. On our way back we come across a party of young people who are still tailgating—three hours after the game has ended—and tossing a football around. "Hey, it's Bart Starr and Brett Favre," a boy calls out, motioning us to pose for a photo. We can't figure out why he says that, since we are wearing Packer gear, but no images or numbers that evoke the legendary quarterbacks. *Maybe, in the Rodgers era, this is his reference for "old." Or maybe he's just drunk.*

Then the one with the football cocks his arm and looks at us quizzically. "Throw it to her," I say, pointing to Carla. "She used to be really good."

The young man tosses the ball to Carla, and she catches it. When she returns it, he throws it again. This one slips through her hands, and she winces in embarrassment. She picks it up and slings it back, and he looks at me.

"Make it easy on the old lady," I tell him. He lobs it gently. I catch the football and pull it into my body as I was taught. It's the first time I've held one since my son was small, and I relish the feel of its pebbled surface. Then I spread my fingers carefully across the laces and manage to put just the hint of a spiral on the ball as I sail it back through the growing twilight.

AT THE END OF THE EARTH

I was tempted to end my story with that ball spiraling into the evening sky. I could have lived in that moment for eternity. But our journey has two days to go.

For some reason we've never done it before, so Monday morning we take the official stadium tour. Our friendly guide, a retired high school coach, takes us to parts of the stadium we've never seen—the inside of a luxury box, a room people rent for weddings. We wind up in the tunnel from which the Packers run onto the field. The guide tells us to imagine uniform numbers on our chests. I channel Hornung's number five, and I swear I'm suddenly standing taller, my padded shoulders broad and my hips narrow. Then the guide plays a recording, the same one we heard at yesterday's game:

"Ladies and gentlemen, we now present ... the twelve-time World Champion ... GREEN ... BAY... PACKERS!"

And we trot out to the field. "Did you feel chills?" our guide asks. We all nod.

After lunch at Titletown Brewery, we cross Dousman Street to the new West Side home of the Neville Public Museum. There's a huge collection of photos there, many from the *Press-Gazette* files, and I have an appointment to select a few for the book. I had expected to slip away and accomplish this chore, but my friends want to see the collection. They coo over shots of the old downtown and ask the curator if there are any pictures of their dads. Del buys several photos of her late father, saying she's never seen those images before.

Late in the afternoon, we pull up to the Porters' cottage near Sturgeon Bay. For the past few years, we've extended each trip with a couple of days at the cottage. As Carla unlocks the door, I catch Pam's eye. We wrinkle our noses at the combined smells of wood smoke and dampness. But we appreciate what this place means to Carla. Her parents bought the land in 1963, and the cottage was first habitable in '66, the year Carla graduated from high school. She has brought her boyfriends and her husbands and her children to this place, and now her children bring their children. *And the ultimate ...* Carla stood here on the beach this past summer as her son and his wife renewed their vows after ten years of marriage. Among the assembled family members were the couple's three children and Carla's eighty-nine-year-old father.

And this is a fine cottage after all, filled with knotty planks and paneling, maritime art, and pictures of Porters at all ages. It has a full kitchen, three bedrooms, and a loft. The spacious living room sports a fireplace flanked by shelves that overflow with books and games. The front of the cottage is mostly windows, looking out on Lake Michigan.

Unlike many gatherings of people over sixty, my friends and I haven't spent a lot of time discussing our health. Pam is running morning blood sugars in the 250 range, but admits lack of exercise is a big part of the problem. We urge her to start a program and to visit her doctor when she gets home. I am having a different sort of issue. Temporary crowns on my upper teeth have decided to become too temporary. I can't go anywhere without denture adhesive in my purse. On Saturday I lost a battle with the crusty bun on a Kroll's cheeseburger. I excused myself for a few minutes and then returned to finish the delectable thing with knife and fork.

Monday night we have dinner with Carla's father and his charming second wife. We are delighted to see Carl Porter still erect and handsome, talking of buying a bigger boat. I use the restroom, and as I flush, something splashes into the toilet. I quickly retrieve the car keys that have fallen from my pocket, but for a few horrible seconds, I'm afraid I've lost my teeth. I share this with my friends, and it provides merriment for the rest of our stay. *Some people are too easily amused.*

On Tuesday, at the suggestion of Carla's stepmother, we view an exhibit of Door County paintings at a gallery in Sturgeon Bay. Pam initially says she's not interested in art, but when I remind her Del will love it, she quickly acquiesces. That exhibit sets the tone for our day. I haven't spent enough time in Door County to succumb to its magic, but I can see why so many do. The county—occupying most of the "thumb" of Wisconsin's mitten—takes its name from a hazardous strait at its northern tip, once known as "Death's Door." It's a place of mists and ghosts on the water; shipping and shipwrecks; hard-working Frenchmen, Germans, and Belgians; tiny towns snuggled into safe harbors. The paintings capture it all.

We leave the exhibit and head up the peninsula. We stop for lunch at a trendy, new bistro in Egg Harbor, but dessert is ice cream at Wilson's in Ephraim, where Del worked as a dishwasher the summer she met Todd.

As we proceed north, I become uncharacteristically irritated with Carla. This is so uncharacteristic, in fact, that I can't recall *in almost fifty years there must have been, but no, not even when she kept my purse* another instance when I've been annoyed with her. She is driving, and she's taking an inordinate amount of time looking for a particular stretch of winding road where she wants to snap a photo. This section of road is often photographed; it's a classic Door County scene. Carla took a picture there last year, but she wants to recapture it with this year's fall foliage. The hang-up is that she doesn't remember the exact location of the scenic road. We shuttle back and forth across the peninsula's northern stretches. The landscape turns from rocky and picturesque to marshy and desolate, and as I fidget in the backseat, I imagine that I'm about to fall off the earth. We're supposed to meet two friends, women we've all known most of our lives, for an early dinner, but Carla won't commit to the plans until she's gotten her shot. We reach Gills Rock, the tip of Wisconsin's thumb, and now I really feel that I have come to the end of the earth.

But as we backtrack, we drive around a curve, and suddenly there is the piece of road in all its undulating perfection. Carla pulls over, scrambles out of the car, clicks the shutter a couple of times, and my irritation is instantly gone. We make dinner with plenty of time to spare, and in the restaurant we find for sale a hanging, metal frog *(Grenouilles!)* that will be perfect for my next birthday gift to Carla. Her birthday is months away, but I buy it on the spot, and she tucks it away in the trunk of her car to take home. "Don't let me forget I got this already!" I tell her, only half joking, aware that I wouldn't have forgotten a few years ago, but I might now.

The next morning at breakfast, Del asks if I'd like an apple. I can't bite into one with my loose teeth, so she cuts tiny pieces off her big honeycrisp and pushes them across the kitchen counter to me. The tender gesture tickles me; I feel like a baby bird. I realize that Todd's arrival is imminent and give Del an especially tight hug as I bid her good-bye. She's nervous, understandably. When she and Todd last saw each other, they were rounding twenty and beautiful in the way that all healthy, young animals are beautiful. Now they are grandparents. *Will there be any chemistry? Will he be kind to her? Will he even keep his promise to show up?*

(Once she's back in California, Del e-mails to say that she and Todd had an interesting time, but that he's not the person with whom she wants to spend the rest of her life. I smile broadly, though, as I read, "Sex was good.")

As we say our farewells, I'm still not sure how I want to end the book, so I put the question to my friends. Just like that. *"I need an ending for my story. So ... the last fifty years ... what was important? What does it all mean?"* I'm expecting someone to say something about football, but instead their replies are all about camaraderie.

Pam thinks a minute and says, "When we get together, we open each other up to new things. I'm not an art person, but you made me go to that exhibit, and I enjoyed it."

"We went our separate ways," Del adds, "but when we get together, we're okay."

Carla poses the question, "How many people our age, who aren't related, get together like this?"

And Pam sums up, "Doing things together, that's the important thing—but you can't get this one bitch to walk!"

We've said our good-byes, but Pam and I linger, reluctant to let go of our precious time with the others. If I were to say that returning to Wisconsin with these women makes me feel young again, it would be both a cliché and a lie. Rather, I search the dear faces for signs of aging. *A downy cheek, a puckered chin—yes, these are like mine.* "I can do this," I tell myself. "This friendship is one of the great things that gets me through the confusing journey we call life. I'm getting old, but I'm in good company."

Carla said it best, earlier on that final, bright blue morning, as we took one last hike to the nearby pier. Out there, surrounded by the wind and the gulls and the water, I thanked her for bringing us to the cottage. "It's neat that we can come up here," I told her.

"The longer we do it and the older we get," she replied, "the neater it's going to be."

ACKNOWLEDGMENTS

Thanks to all who helped this late-blooming rookie author.

To the women I've renamed Pam Monaghan, Del LeBlanc, and Carla Porter, for allowing me to use your personal histories and recount some embarrassing moments. I love you, and I hope we all have a lot more years to reconnect in Green Bay.

To C. Linda Dowell for images from an older Green Bay.

To Louise Pfotenhauer, Curator of Collections, Neville Public Museum of Brown County, for helping me to locate additional photos to illustrate my story, and to Charles "Chip" Manthey for leading me to Louise.

To my beloved son, the horror-movie *maven,* for his encouragement. *May we both succeed in our creative endeavors.*

To the following who read the manuscript at various stages and made comments or suggestions: Myra Cristall, Sandy Elliott, Madeleine Fern, Carolyn Haude, Jean Kandel, Joyce Laughlin, Kathleen LeBlanc, David Nagy, Judy Paulson, Holly Phillips, Stacy Recker, Cynthia Taubert, Cathy Vengen, Jim Wallace, Holly Wilcox. Special thanks to Myra (the small-detail person), Stacy, Kathleen, Cindy, and Holly W. for taking the time to write down their comments.

And for their less specific, but nonetheless appreciated, support: Adrienne Baach, Wendy Burkett, Ginny Buzzell, Marilyn Freimuth, Jarrie Haltaufderheid, Mary Mezera, Elizabeth Megan Mosier, Marilyn Nagy, Stacia Nagy, Carolyn Rafales. And thanks to friends from Save the Animals Foundation, too numerous to mention. (I'd hate to leave anyone out.) Special thanks to Marilyn F., who elaborated the benefits of self-publishing, and to Megan, who first told me about supported self-publishing.

Kudos to Mick Trick of Save the Animals Foundation for endorsing this project even though she knows that if the book is to be successful, it might take me away from STAF for a time.

To Mari Beth Jacobs of Studio 7 salon, and to Jeremy Borsky, DDS, and his assistant Erin Lippmeier, for allowing me to try out my material on them as I sat in their chairs and they rendered me fit to appear in public. *Special mention to Dr. Borsky for informing me that Vince Lombardi had a class 3 jaw.*

To Monica Dias of Frost Brown Todd LLC, Cincinnati, OH, for providing guidelines on the legal ramifications of publishing a memoir. *If someone throws a flag, blame me, not Monica.*

And a big thanks to the staff of iUniverse for their expert guidance.

REFERENCES

The following works are quoted or referenced in the text of *Incomplete Passes:*

Alexander, Ronald. *Time Out for Ginger.* First produced at the Lyceum Theatre on Broadway on November 26, 1952. Copyright 1948, 1953, by Ronald Alexander; renewed 1976 by Ronald Alexander under the title *Season for Ginger.*

Da Yoopers. *Deer Hunter's Widow.* From the album *Camp Fever.* Recorded for You Guys, 1988.

Doctor Zhivago. MGM, 1965. Directed by David Lean and starring Omar Sharif and Julie Christie. Based on the novel by Boris Pasternak, first English translation by Pantheon Books, New York, 1958.

Dylan, Bob. *The Times They Are a-Changin'.* Recorded for Columbia Records. Released in January 1964.

Goldfinger. MGM,1964. Directed by Guy Hamilton and starring Sean Connery, Gert Frobe, and Honor Blackman. Based on the novel by Ian Fleming, published by Jonathan Cape, London, 1959.

Hopkin, Mary. *Those Were the Days.* Melody is supposedly a Russian Gypsy song. English lyrics by Gene Raskin, 1962. Recorded for Apple Records, 1968.

Hornung, Paul, as told to William F. Reed. *Golden Boy: Girls, Games, and Gambling at Green Bay (and Notre Dame, Too)*. New York: Simon & Schuster, 2004.

Keillor, Garrison. *A Prairie Home Companion*. Minnesota Public Radio and other public radio stations.

Knowles, John. *A Separate Peace*. New York: Scribner, 1959; copyright renewed 1987.

Kramer, Jerry, with Dick Schaap. *Distant Replay*. New York: G. P. Putnam's Sons, 1985.

Maraniss, David. *When Pride Still Mattered: A Life of Vince Lombardi*. New York: Simon & Schuster, 1999.

Shepherd, Jean. *A Christmas Story*. Based on his semi-autobiographical short stories and anecdotes. Directed by Bob Clark and starring Peter Billingsley, Melinda Dillon, and Darren McGavin. Warner Brothers, 1983.

Sondheim, Stephen. Lyrics for *West Side Story*. Originally performed on Broadway in 1957. Script by Arthur Laurents. Music by Leonard Bernstein. Directed and choreographed by Jerome Robbins and produced by Robert E. Griffith and Harold Prince.

Taylor, Jim, with Kristine Setting Clark. *The Fire Within*. Chicago: Triumph Books, 2010.

For checking game dates and scores, the following websites have been invaluable:
http://www.packers.com and http://www.pro-football-reference.com.

Made in the USA
Lexington, KY
14 December 2011